WINDOWS 95

FOR

DUMMIES®

Quick Reference

2nd Edition

WINDOWS® 95 FOR DUMMIES®

Quick Reference
2nd Edition

by Greg Harvey

IDG
BOOKS
WORLDWIDE

IDG Books Worldwide, Inc.
An International Data Group Company

Foster City, CA ✦ Chicago, IL ✦ Indianapolis, IN ✦ Southlake, TX

Windows® 95 For Dummies® Quick Reference, 2nd Edition

Published by
IDG Books Worldwide, Inc.
An International Data Group Company
919 E. Hillsdale Blvd.
Suite 400
Foster City, CA 94404

Library of Congress Catalog Card No.: 95-81244

ISBN: 1-56884-981-8

Printed in the United States of America

10 9 8 7 6 5 4 3 2

2H/QW/QT/ZW/IN

Distributed in the United States by IDG Books Worldwide, Inc.

Distributed by Macmillan Canada for Canada; by Computer and Technical Books for the Caribbean Basin; by Contemporanea de Ediciones for Venezuela; by Distribuidora Cuspide for Argentina; by CITEC for Brazil; by Ediciones ZETA S.C.R. Ltda. for Peru; by Editorial Limusa SA for Mexico; by Transworld Publishers Limited in the United Kingdom and Europe; by Al-Maiman Publishers & Distributors for Saudi Arabia; by Simron Pty. Ltd. for South Africa; by IDG Communications (HK) Ltd. for Hong Kong; by Toppan Company Ltd. for Japan; by Addison Wesley Publishing Company for Korea; by Longman Singapore Publishers Ltd. for Singapore, Malaysia, Thailand, and Indonesia; by Unalis Corporation for Taiwan; by WS Computer Publishing Company, Inc. for the Philippines; by WoodsLane Pty. Ltd. for Australia; by WoodsLane Enterprises Ltd. for New Zealand.

For general information on IDG Books Worldwide's books in the U.S., please call our Consumer Customer Service department at 800-762-2974. For reseller information, including discounts and premium sales, please call our Reseller Customer Service department at 800-434-3422.

For information on where to purchase IDG Books Worldwide's books outside the U.S., contact IDG Books Worldwide at 415-655-3021 or fax 415-655-3295.

For information on translations, contact Marc Jeffrey Mikulich, Director, Foreign & Subsidiary Rights, at IDG Books Worldwide, 415-655-3018 or fax 415-655-3295.

For sales inquiries and special prices for bulk quantities, write to the address above or call IDG Books Worldwide at 415-655-3200.

For information on using IDG Books Worldwide's books in the classroom, or ordering examination copies, contact the Education Office at 800-434-2086 or fax 817-251-8174.

For authorization to photocopy items for corporate, personal, or educational use, please contact Copyright Clearance Center, 222 Rosewood Drive, Danvers, MA 01923, or fax 508-750-4470.

is a trademark under exclusive license to IDG Books Worldwide, Inc., from International Data Group, Inc.

About the Author

Greg Harvey

Greg Harvey, the author of over 30 computer books, has been training business people in the use of IBM PC, DOS, and software application programs such as WordPerfect, Lotus 1-2-3, and dBASE since 1983. He has written numerous training manuals, user guides, and books for business users of software. He currently teaches Lotus 1-2-3 and dBASE courses in the Department of Information Systems at Golden Gate University in San Francisco. Harvey is the author of *Excel For Dummies, Excel for Windows 95 For Dummies, 1-2-3 For Dummies, PC World WordPerfect 6 Handbook, DOS For Dummies Quick Reference,* and *WordPerfect For Dummies Quick Reference,* all from IDG Books Worldwide, Inc.

Acknowledgments

A very special thank you to Michael Bryant for suffering through the incomplete Windows 95 betas and practically nonexistent documentation to make sense out of many of the more obscure features and to create the figures for this book ("You're the greatest, pal!").

I want to thank the following people at IDG Books as well, who worked so hard to make this book a reality:

David Solomon and John Kilcullen for their support for this "baby" Dummies book.

Brandon Nordin and Milissa Koloski for coming up with the original concept of quick references for the rest of us.

Megg Bonar for straightening out all the contract details and just being her usual, great self!

Diane Steele for making this project possible and supporting me all the way.

Pamela Mourouzis, Diane Giangrossi, Diana Conover, and Jennifer Ehrlich for their inspired editorial assistance.

Rob Rubright for the tech review and Beth Jenkins and the amazing layout folks in Production.

Last, but never least, I want to acknowledge my indebtedness to Dan Gookin, whose vision, sardonic wit, and (sometimes) good humor produced *DOS For Dummies,* the "Mother" of all */...For Dummies* books. Thanks for the inspiration and the book that made it all possible, Dan.

Greg Harvey
Inverness, California

(The publisher would like to thank Patrick J. McGovern, without whom this book would not have been possible.)

Credits

**Senior Vice President
and Publisher**
Milissa L. Koloski

Associate Publisher
Diane Graves Steele

Brand Manager
Judith A. Taylor

Editorial Managers
Kristin A. Cocks
Mary Corder

**Product Development
Manager**
Mary Bednarek

**Editorial Executive
Assistant**
Richard Graves

Editorial Assistants
Constance Carlisle
Chris Collins
Kevin Spencer

Production Director
Beth Jenkins

Production Assistant
Jacalyn L. Pennywell

**Supervisor of
Project Coordination**
Cindy L. Phipps

Supervisor of Page Layout
Kathie S. Schnorr

**Supervisor of Graphics
and Design**
Shelley Lea

**Reprint/Blueline
Coordination**
Tony Augsburger
Patricia R. Reynolds
Todd Klemme
Theresa Sánchez-Baker

**Media/Archive
Coordination**
Leslie Popplewell
Melissa Stauffer
Jason Marcuson

Project Editors
Pamela Mourouzis
Jennifer Ehrlich

Editors
Diana R. Conover
Diane L. Giangrossi

Editorial Assistants
Constance Carlisle
Chris Collins
Kevin Spencer

Technical Reviewers
Rob Rubright
Victor Robert Garza

Project Coordinator
Valery Bourke

Graphics Coordination
Gina Scott
Angela F. Hunckler
Carla Radzikinas

Production Page Layout
Shawn Alysworth
Elizabeth Cárdenas-Nelson
Jill Lyttle
Jane Martin

Proofreaders
Mary C. Oby
Christine Meloy Beck
Gwenette Gaddis
Dwight Ramsey
Robert Springer

Indexer
David Heiret

Cover Design
Kavish + Kavish

Contents at a Glance

Table of Contents

Part III: Doing Everyday Junk in Windows 95 .. 73

How to Use This Book

Welcome to *Windows 95 For Dummies Quick Reference,*
2nd Edition — a quick reference that looks at the lighter
side of Windows 95 features and tasks. This book not
only gives you the lowdown on Windows 95, but it does
so in a way that is quick and easy-to-use.

You've heard of on-line help. Well, just think of this book
as on-side help. Keep it by your side when you're at the
computer, and before you try to perform a Windows 95
task that you're the least bit unsure of, look it up in the
appropriate section. Scan the entry, looking for any
warnings (those nasty bomb icons). Afterwards, simply
follow the steps to guide you through the options.

The Cast of Icons

In your travels through this book, you'll come across the following icons:

A tip to make you a more clever Windows 95 user.

Look out! Something in this task can get you into trouble.

A handy-dandy guide to point you straight to the sections in *Windows 95 For Dummies* where you can find more examples of how to use this command or perform this task.

Highlights features that may not work as you would typically expect.

Indicates the quickest possible way to accomplish a certain task under normal circumstances.

How This Book is Organized

For your convenience, this book is divided into five parts:

+ Part I: Getting to Know Windows 95

+ Part II: The Basic Stuff in Windows 95

+ Part III: Doing Everyday Junk in Windows 95

+ Part IV: Accessories for Every Appetite

+ Part V: Control Panel City

Each of these sections contains the various features and tasks that you may need to use as you journey into the world of Windows 95. To make this book easier for you to follow, each Windows 95 feature and task is listed in alphabetical order and handled in a similar way:

+ Following the name, you'll find a brief description of the function.

+ The "How do I get to it?" and "What do I do with it?" sections appear below the description. Here, you find the "more answers, less reading" part of the book. You can follow the steps you need to get to a certain feature and do something useful with it. In most cases, you will find that the "How do I get to it?" section shows you in a "picturesque" sequence how to access a feature or accomplish a task.

✦ Following the "What do I do with it?" section, in some cases, you'll find an "Isn't there another way?" section that gives you yet another variation for getting at a particular feature in Windows 95.

✦ Bringing up the rear, you'll find a "More stuff" section, where I stick in any tips, warnings, reminders, or other trivia that just might come in handy while you're roaming around this area of Windows.

Miscellaneous Information

This book is designed for beginners who have at least some experience with Windows in the 3.0 or 3.1 varieties, but who have never had a gander at all the new stuff in Windows 95. If you are really a greenhorn when it comes to Windows 95, glance over Part I, "Getting to Know Windows 95," and Part II, "The Basic Stuff in Windows 95." If you can't find enough information to help you there, then please get your hands on a copy of Andy Rathbone's excellent *Windows 95 For Dummies,* which is a much more extensive reference and provides a good starting point for learning about Windows 95.

Following are some other bits of information that will help you to navigate your way around this book:

✦ To make it easier for you to go back and forth between the telegraphic information presented in this quick reference and in *Windows 95 For Dummies,* I've cross-referenced some topics to related discussions in that book. (Look for the Cross-Reference icons.)

✦ If I think that it will be helpful for you to refer to another section of this book, I include a ***See also*** note with the appropriate section listed.

✦ If I mention a term that you aren't familiar with, don't panic. Simply turn to the back of this book and look the term up in the Glossary that I have provided for emergencies such as these.

Part 1

Getting to Know Windows 95

If you're an old pro at using Windows, then this part probably won't be worth your while. But if you're new to the Windows scene, stick around awhile — you just might come away from this with some new information about how to make your time spent with Windows 95 as painless as possible.

Most of the features of Windows 95 are discussed at length in the body of this book. However, some of the very basics should be squared away up front. With this in mind, this part gives you the run-down on strange words like *click* and *double-click* so you can get up and running with Windows 95.

In this part . . .

- ✔ **Understanding menus**
- ✔ **Understanding windows (the on-screen type)**
- ✔ **Using the keyboard**
- ✔ **Using the mouse**

Understanding Menus

Windows 95 is full of different kinds of menus, which are described more fully in the body of this book. However, it is helpful to understand a few general rules when using the various menus:

✦ If you see a right-facing arrowhead (>) to the right of an option on a menu, another menu full of more options appears when you highlight (or select) that option.

✦ If you see an ellipsis (. . .) at the end of an option in a menu, a dialog box full of check boxes, text boxes, and such appears when you select that option.

✦ If you don't see any kind of symbol next to an option in a menu, it is pretty safe to assume that once you select that option the command will be carried out immediately.

Understanding Windows (The On-Screen Type)

Put simply, a *window* is a little box on-screen that you can modify in many different ways.

✦ You can change the size of a window by dragging its borders with the mouse or by using the Size command (**see also** "Control Menu" in Part II of this book).

✦ You can move windows around by dragging them or by using the Move command (**see also** "Control Menu" in Part II of this book).

✦ You can turn windows into little buttons on the taskbar at the bottom of the Windows 95 screen by using the Minimize command (**see also** "Control Menu" in Part II of this book).

✦ You can make windows fill the entire screen by using the Maximize command (**see also** "Control Menu" in Part II of this book).

✦ You can change windows to an in-between size by using the Restore command (**see also** "Control Menu" in Part II of this book).

✦ You can completely close windows by using the Close command (**see also** "Control Menu" in Part II of this book).

Using the Keyboard

I know that many of you are old-line defenders of the keyboard and would rather keep rodents off of your desktops. Well, that's okay with me. The truth is that some chores you'll find yourselves doing in Windows 95 are quicker and easier to accomplish by using the keyboard. For this reason, I've thrown in the following table to show you some basic pointers about keyboard usage.

Key	What happens when you press it
Esc	The Escape key's job is to get you out of predicaments. If you find yourself in an unfamiliar menu or dialog box when using Windows 95, pressing Esc backs you out.
F1 – F12	When you use these keys — called *function keys* — either alone or in combination with the Shift and Ctrl keys, you can get things done quickly.
Print Scrn, Scroll Lock, and Pause	These keys used to do something useful in the olden days of personal computing, but they don't have much use any more. It's probably safe to ignore them.
Insert	When you press this key, you go into Insert mode where the text that you type replaces any text that may be to the right of your insertion point. Press it again and you're back to regular mode, where the text you type scoots all existing text to the right, but leaves it intact.
Home	When you press this key, your insertion point moves over to the left margin.
Page Up	When you press this key, the insertion point moves up one screenful.
Page Down	When you press this key, the insertion point moves down one screenful.
Delete	When you press this key, you erase the character to the right of the insertion point. You can also use this key to erase any words, files, or various other elements that you've selected.
End	When you press this key, your insertion point moves over to the right margin.
Enter	When you press this key, you add a line to your text and place the insertion point in it or complete a command if you're selecting from a menu. This key can also be used to give the go-ahead so Windows 95 will accept the information that you've added to a dialog box or edit box.
Num Lock	When you press this key, the keyboard is set so that the numeric keypad types only numbers. Press it again if you want to use the directional arrows and other cursor movement keys found on the numeric keypad.
↑ ↓ ← →	When you press these *arrow keys,* the insertion point moves in the appropriate direction.

Key	What happens when you press it
Ctrl	You can take lots of shortcuts by pressing the Control key along with various other keys.
Alt	You can use the *Alternate* key much like you can use the Ctrl key. The Alt key, however, has one other job: You can press it along with *hotkeys* — those underlined letters that you sometimes see in menus and dialog boxes — to do a job quickly without reaching for the mouse.
Shift	This key, like it's predecessor on the old typewriters, changes lowercase letters to uppercase letters. This key can also be used in conjunction with the Ctrl key to create various key combinations that make your work faster and easier.
Caps Lock	When you press this key, you can type in all uppercase letters without having to hold down the Shift key. In order to type those symbols above the numbers on the top row of your keyboard, however, you still have to press Shift.

Using the Mouse

The mouse is that little hand-held pointing device that you use to input information into your computer. Sometimes Windows 95 requires you to use the mouse in different ways in order to accomplish different goals.

Click

Clicking is probably the most common mouse action. Clicking simply means that you point at an object and then press and quickly release the *primary mouse button.* The primary mouse button is usually the left one, but some of you left-handers may have a mouse that uses the right button as the primary one. Either way, the primary mouse button is usually the inmost button, closest to your keyboard.

This book often uses the words *choose* and *select,* which can be substituted for the word *click.*

Double-click

To double-click is to press and release the primary mouse button (described above) two times in rapid succession without moving the mouse between clicks. You often use this action to open programs and such from icons.

Secondary-click

To secondary-click is to press and release the button that is not designated as your primary mouse button (usually the right mouse button unless you're a lefty and have switched the buttons). This action often brings up context menus and other goodies.

Drag

Dragging is a little bit different, but it still uses the same principles of clicking. In order to drag an object, you must first point to it with the mouse pointer; then click and hold down the primary mouse button and move the mouse to drag the object to the position on-screen that you want. Finally, let go of the mouse button. This action is quite useful for such chores as rearranging icons or moving files to the Recycle Bin.

Part II

The Basic Stuff in Windows 95

In some ways operating systems are like junkyards littered with all kinds of seemingly unrelated stuff that you have to make sense of. This part of the book contains an alphabetical listing of all the fundamental stuff from Accessories to Wizards that you'll surely encounter when wandering around the operating system junkyard known as Windows 95. Here, you'll get the lowdown on important Windows 95 stuff like the things mentioned in the following list:

In this part . . .

✔ **In what context do you use context menus?**

✔ **How do you have an intelligent conversation with a dialog box?**

✔ **What kinds of things can you find with the Explorer?**

✔ **Just how long are long filenames anyway?**

✔ **What should you do if you're in the Network Neighborhood?**

✔ **What's the most ecological way to get rid of stuff in the Recycle Bin?**

✔ **Just what are the tasks of the taskbar?**

. . . and much, much more.

Accessories

Accessories are little programs that come with Windows 95. Accessories aren't really necessary to run your computer, but they're sometimes handy to have around. These mini-programs run the gamut from fun stuff like Games and Multimedia to yucky stuff like Direct Cable Connection and Dial-Up Networking.

How do I get to it?

To open any of the Windows accessories, you follow these steps:

1. Click [Start] on the taskbar.

2. Click [Programs] on the Start menu.

3. Click [Accessories] on the Program's continuation menu.

4. Choose the name of the desired accessory on the long Accessories continuation menu; then click the primary mouse button to open the program's dialog box.

In the case of the Fax, Games, Multimedia, and System Tools, you have to navigate over and down one more level of menus to select the actual game, multimedia program, or system utility that you want to open.

Here you see the choices that you have when you select Games on the Accessories continuation menu:

What do I do with it?

Windows 95 contains a wide variety of accessories, some of which (like the Hearts and Minesweeper games) you'll use more than others (like Character Map and Direct Cable Connection). Part IV gives you a rundown on the accessories included with Windows 95 in alphabetical order.

Isn't there another way?

The only way to open your favorite accessory is by going through the Start-menu-to-Programs-menu-to-Accessories-menu rigmarole unless you create a shortcut for the program and place it on the desktop.

If you create shortcuts for your favorite accessory program, you can then just double-click the shortcut icon for that program on the desktop and, presto, Windows opens it (*see* "Shortcuts" later in this part for information on how you'd do so). How's that for no more fumbling around with continuation menus?

More stuff

After you open your accessory's dialog box, remember that you can often get help on using the utility either by choosing a topic from the Help pull-down menu in the dialog box or clicking the ? button on the dialog box's title bar.

Context Menus

Context (also known as *shortcut*) menus are pull-down menus that just contain a bunch of commands directly related to the object to which they are attached.

How do I get to it?

To open a context menu, you must click the object with the secondary mouse button.

If you don't know your secondary mouse button from the primary mouse button, here's how you can tell which is which:

1. Move the mouse pointer to the center of the desktop (where it's not on top of anything else, like an icon or open window).

2. Click one of the mouse buttons.

If nothing happens, you just clicked the primary mouse button (the one you use to select objects and menu items in Windows 95). If, however, a little menu starting with Arrange Icons and ending with Properties appears, then you just clicked the secondary mouse button (used to open context menus like the one you're looking at).

TIP

You can switch which button is the primary button (for normal select and drag) and which is the secondary button (for context menus) with the Mouse icon in the Control Panel (*see* "Mouse" in Part V for more information on doing so).

In the following figure, you see the context menu associated with the hard disk icon in the My Computer window. To open this context menu on the lower right of the Hard disk (C:) icon, I simply clicked the icon with the secondary mouse button.

What do I do with it?

Once you've opened a context menu, you can choose any of its commands just like you would with any regulation pull-down menu:

✦ Drag up or down to highlight the command and then click it with the primary mouse button (or release the button if you drag with the mouse button pressed).

✦ Type its hotkey (the letter in the command that's underlined).

✦ Press the ↑ or ↓ key to highlight the command and then press Enter to choose it.

Almost all context menus attached to program, folder, and file icons on the desktop or in a window let you choose commands that do stuff like open the object, create a shortcut for it (*see* "Shortcuts" later in Part II), and get the lowdown on it (*see* "Properties" later in Part II).

Most context menus attached to the windows themselves have commands that let you do stuff like change the size of the icons in a window (*see* "Changing the View Options for a Window" in Part III) and change the order in which the window's icons are displayed (*see* "Arranging the Icons in a Window" in Part III).

Other common things that an object's context menu commands may let you do (depending upon the object in question) are as follows:

✦ Explore the contents of the object (*see* "Explorer" later in Part II)

✦ Cut or copy the object to the Clipboard so that the object can be moved or copied to another place on your system or network (*see* "Copying Files and Folders" in Part III)

✦ Delete the object by putting it into the Recycle Bin (*see* "Deleting Junk" in Part III)

✦ Send a copy of the object to a fax machine (*see* "Microsoft Exchange" later in Part II) or a specific floppy drive (*see* "Copying Files and Folders" in Part III)

Beyond the common stuff, you may run into very specialized commands that relate only to the function of that particular object in Windows 95. For example, on the taskbar's context menu, you find such specialized commands as Cascade, Tile Horizontally, Tile Vertically, and Minimize All Windows for controlling how all the open windows shown on the taskbar are arranged on the desktop (*see* "Taskbar" later in Part II).

More stuff

See also "Pull-Down Menus" and "Toolbar," later in Part II, for other ways to select commands in Windows 95.

Control Menu

The Control Menu is a standard pull-down menu attached to all the windows that you'll ever open in Windows 95. The commands on this pull-down menu do simple things like resize, relocate, and close the window to which it's attached.

How do I get to it?

To open the Control Menu on any window in Windows 95, click the little icon to the immediate left of the window's name in the upper-left corner of the window's title bar.

If you double-click this icon instead of single-clicking it, Windows closes the window (and quits any application program that happens to be running in it). If your window suddenly goes "poof" on you, then that's just what you did. Don't worry: if you had any unsaved documents open in the program whose window you just closed, Windows 95 will so warn you and give you a chance to save them before the window becomes toast.

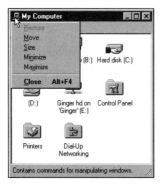

What do I do with it?

Almost every Control Menu you run into has these same old tired commands on them:

Common Menu Commands	What They Do
Restore	This command restores — hence the name — a maximized or minimized window back to an in-between size that you can easily change (***see*** "Move," next).
Move	This command lets you move the window to a new location on the desktop. When you select Move, the mouse pointer changes from an arrow to a double-cross. At that point, all you need to do is press an arrow key (which changes the pointer from a double-cross to a standard arrow) so that you can then relocate the window by moving the mouse pointer or by continuing to press the appropriate arrow keys.
	Once you have the window where you want it, click the mouse pointer somewhere on the desktop or press Enter to set the window down in its new location.
	If you want to bail on moving the window before setting it down in a new location on the desktop, press Esc and the window returns to its original position.

Common Menu Commands	What They Do
Size	This command lets you resize the window by moving its left, right, top, or bottom side. This action is very similar to moving a window, except that it allows you to change the vertical or horizontal size of the window by selecting one of the arrow keys and then moving the mouse or pressing the appropriate arrow key.
Minimize	This command shrinks the window all the way down to a button on the taskbar at the bottom of the screen.
Maximize	This command zooms the window to full size so that it fills up the entire screen.
Close (Alt+F4)	This command closes the window, thus automatically exiting the program running in it.

Isn't there another way?

However convenient the Control Menu commands may seem at first blush, Windows 95 offers some easier sizing and moving alternatives in the form of the following specialized buttons and mouse techniques:

✦ To shrink the window down to a button on the taskbar, click the ▣ button on the right side of the window's title bar.

✦ To zoom the window up to full size, click the ▣ button on the right side of the window's title bar.

✦ To restore a maximized window to its former size, click the ▣ button that replaces the Maximize button.

✦ To close the window and exit any program running in it, click the ☒ button on the right side of the window's title bar.

✦ To restore a minimized window that's part of the taskbar to its former size and position, click its button on the taskbar.

✦ To move a window on the desktop, position the mouse pointer somewhere on the window's title bar and drag the outline to the new location with the mouse.

✦ To resize a window in one direction, position the mouse pointer somewhere on one of the window's sides; when the pointer changes to a double-headed arrow, drag the window's outline to the desired size with the mouse.

✦ To resize a window in two directions at one time, position the mouse pointer on one of the window's four corners. When the pointer changes to a diagonal double-headed arrow, drag the window's outline to the desired size with the mouse.

For pre-Windows 95 users only

If you've been using earlier versions of Windows (like 3.1 and 3.0), you may have noticed that the Switch To command that was used to open the Task List dialog box is missing from the Windows 95 Control Menu. The reason for this omission is that Windows 95 no longer contains the Task List dialog box (if you press Ctrl+Esc, the old keystroke shortcut for opening the Task List dialog box in Windows 3.1, the Start menu simply pops up as though you had clicked the Start button on the taskbar).

Instead of using the Task List dialog box to switch between open windows as in previous versions of Windows, you now use the taskbar (*see* "Taskbar" later in Part II for the details).

More stuff

See also "Windows," later in Part II, for the lowdown on other parts of the typical window.

Control Panel

The Control Panel contains a wide selection of icons that let you customize the Windows 95 settings on your computer.

How do I get to it?

To open the Control Panel, follow these steps:

1. Click 🏁Start on the taskbar.

2. Choose 🗂 Settings ▸ on the Start menu.

3. Choose 📟 Control Panel ▸ on the Settings continuation menu.

When you select Control Panel on the Settings continuation menu, the Control Panel window appears.

What do I do with it?

Once you have the Control Panel open, you can open any of its Properties dialog boxes or windows in one of two ways:

> ✦ Double-click the icon whose settings you want to change.
>
> *or*
>
> ✦ Click the icon with the secondary mouse button to open the icon's shortcut menu and then select the Open command.

Most of the Control Menu icons are attached to Properties dialog boxes, whose options you use to change the settings pertaining to that icon. A few of the icons (like those for Fonts and Printers, which are really just shortcuts) open windows. To change the settings for those icons, you need to use the window's pull-down commands.

Isn't there another way?

You can also open the Control Panel from the My Computer window or the Exploring window.

> ✦ To open the Control Panel from the My Computer window, open the My Computer window and then double-click the Control Panel folder icon in that window.
>
> ✦ To open the Control Panel from the Exploring window, open the Windows Explorer and then drag down to the Control Panel folder in the All Folders pane. Click this Control Panel folder icon to display the Control Panel icons in the Contents of 'Control Panel' pane of the Exploring window.

More stuff

See also "Dialog Box," later in Part II, for more information on how to deal with the options presented by the various Control Panel dialog boxes.

Desktop

The desktop is the background against which all the stuff in Windows 95 takes place. It contains the taskbar, My Computer, Network Neighborhood, and Recycle Bin icons along with any shortcuts you've created and windows and dialog boxes that you've opened.

What do I do with it?

The desktop contains a context menu (***see*** "Context Menu" earlier in Part II if you don't know what this is) that enables you to do the following cool things:

✦ Arrange Icons on the desktop by Name, by Type, by Size, or by Date, or use Auto Arrange to let Windows 95 decide how to arrange them

✦ Line up Icons on the desktop when you seem to have them all over the place and want to put them back in neat columns and rows

✦ Undo Delete when you've just gotten rid of something on the desktop — like a folder or a shortcut — and you want to get it out of the Recycle Bin and put it back on the desktop where it belongs

✦ New to create an empty folder, a file of a particular type (like an Excel 5.0 worksheet, a Word 6.0 document, a sound file, a text document, or a bitmap graphics file), or a briefcase (assuming that you have installed the Briefcase accessory — ***see*** "My Briefcase" in this part), or to create a new shortcut

✦ Properties to open the Display Properties dialog box, where you can select a new background pattern or wallpaper for the desktop and do a number of other display-type things. (***See also*** "Display," in Part V.)

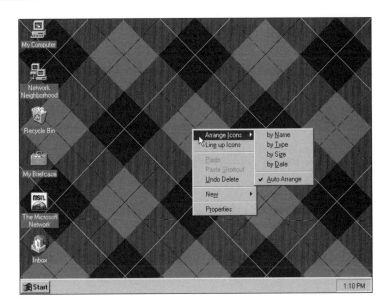

More stuff

See also "Control Menu," earlier in Part II, for information on opening and closing windows on the desktop.

See also "Icons," later in Part II, for more information on icons.

See also "Taskbar," later in Part II, for information on arranging the taskbar on the desktop.

See also "Moving and Resizing Windows," in Part III, for information on moving and resizing windows on the desktop.

Dialog Box

A dialog box is a special type of window that enables you to specify a bunch of settings all at the same time.

How do I get to it?

Most dialog boxes appear as the result of selecting a menu command from either a pull-down menu or a context menu. You can always tell when selecting a pull-down menu command will result in a dialog box: If it will, the command name is followed by an *ellipsis* (that's Greek for three dots in a row).

For example, you know that choosing the Options... command on the View pull-down menu in a Windows 95 window results in a dialog box because the command appears as Options... rather than simply Options (no ellipsis).

Selecting pull-down or context menu commands with ellipses is not the only way to open a dialog box: double-clicking certain icons in the Control Panel also gives you a dialog box of further options (*see* "Control Panel" earlier in Part II).

What do I do with it?

Once you've opened a dialog box, you have to know how to use its various boxes and buttons to make your selections known to Windows 95 or the particular Windows program you have open. Dialog boxes usually contain a combination of the following buttons and boxes:

Parts of a Dialog Box	What You Do with Them
Check box	Used with items that allow you to choose more than one option. Selected options appear with a check mark inside the box, while the current check box option appears with a faint, dotted line around the option name.
	Click the arrow button to open a list box of possible choices. If there are more choices than will fit in the box, use the scroll bar on the right to display more choices.
Command button	Used to initiate an action, such as putting the options you've selected into effect with the OK button.
Drop-down list box	Looks like a text box with a down-arrow button right next door.
Edit (or text) box	Shows you the current setting (usually a filename or directory path) and lets you edit it or type in a whole new setting.
	If the command name is followed by an ellipsis (. . .), choosing the button displays another dialog box. If the command name is followed by two greater-than symbols (> >), choosing the button expands the current dialog box to display more choices. If the command name is dimmed, the button is temporarily off-limits.
	If the text inside the box is selected, anything you type replaces the highlighted text. You can also delete text by pressing the Delete or Backspace key.
List box	Displays an alphabetical list of all choices for an item. Use the scroll bar on the right to display new choices (*see* "Windows" later in Part II for an explanation of scroll bars). The current choice is highlighted in the list.

Parts of a Dialog Box	What You Do with Them
Radio (option) button	Used with items that allow you to choose only one of several options. The selected option appears with a dot in the middle of the radio button and a faint, dotted line around the option name.
Slider	Lets you change a value (such as the volume or mouse speed) by dragging the slider back and forth (usually between Low and High, marked at each end).
Spinner buttons	A pair of buttons, one with an up arrow on top of one with a down arrow, that enable you to select a new number in an accompanying edit box without having to actually type in that edit box. Clicking the up-arrow spinner button increases the value by one, and clicking the down-arrow spinner button decreases it by one.
Tab	Lets you select among related groups of options within the dialog box.

Keep in mind that you can always move a dialog box to a new part of the desktop by dragging it around by its little title bar (*see* "Windows" later in Part II if you don't know a title bar from a title page). Just because you can move a dialog box like other standard windows, don't get it in your head that you can resize dialog boxes as you can regular windows.

More stuff

Remember: You can tell a dialog box from a full-blown window by the title bar: Dialog boxes only have Help and Close buttons in the upper-right corner of the title bar, whereas full-blown windows have Minimize, Maximize, and Close buttons in this part of the title bar. Also, full-blown windows have a menu bar underneath the title bar, a place where many dialog boxes show tabs (*see* "Windows" later in Part II for more stuff on windows).

Explorer

The Windows Explorer lets you view the contents of any part of your system, including the desktop, your entire computer, a particular disk on the computer (such as a $3^{1}/_{2}$-inch floppy in drive A, the hard disk of drive C, or a CD-ROM), or some other special stuff, like the Control Panel, Recycle Bin, My Briefcase, Network Neighborhood, or Printers folders.

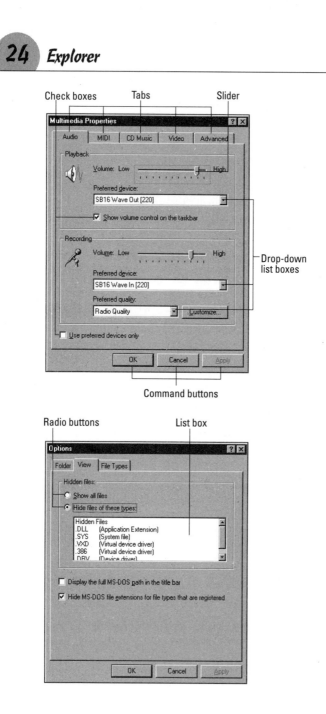

Check boxes   Tabs   Slider

Drop-down list boxes

Command buttons

Radio buttons   List box

How do I get to it?

To open the Exploring window, follow these steps:

1. Click ▦Start on the taskbar.

2. Choose ▦ Programs ▶ on the Start menu.

3. Choose ▨ Windows Explorer on the Programs continuation menu.

When you click Windows Explorer on the Programs continuation menu, Windows opens the Exploring window. This window is divided into panes:

✦ All Folders on the left

✦ Contents of whatever is selected in All Folders on the right

To select a new part of your system to view in the Contents of pane, simply click the icon for that part in the All Folders pane. When you select a disk or a folder in the All Folders pane, the status bar at the bottom of the Exploring window displays the number of objects (that is, files) in that disk or folder on the left side along with the total disk space (in megabytes) used by these objects on the right side.

To view the nether parts of the system in the All Folders pane, use the scroll bar on the right. For example, to see the contents of a folder named New Ventures on your hard disk, you drag the scroll button down until you see the folder called New Ventures; then click its folder icon. Windows immediately displays a listing of all the folders and files that are contained within the New Ventures folder.

When fooling around with the icons in the All Folders pane, you will undoubtedly notice little tiny boxes, with pluses and minuses, at the nexus of the dotted lines that show which things belong to items above (forming a kind of computer organization chart).

✦ When the box has a minus sign in it, clicking the box collapses the list down to just the item to the right of the box, removing from the display everything (folders, for example) contained under that item.

✦ When the box has a plus sign in it, clicking the box expands the list, showing all the things that are contained within the item to the right of the box.

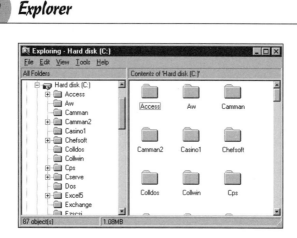

You can use the options on the View pull-down menu to control how the stuff in the Contents of pane of the Exploring window is displayed. Normally, Windows 95 chooses the Large Icons option to make the folders and files appear as large as possible.

✦ If you want to retain the icon look but need to see as much stuff in the Contents of pane as possible, choose Small Icons or the List command on the View menu.

✦ If you need to know junk about the files — such as what types of files they are, their size, or the date they were last modified — select the Details command instead. Keep in mind, however, that the Details viewing option is the biggest space hog, so when selecting this option, you may want to maximize the Exploring window by using the Maximize button or the Maximize command on the Exploring window's Control Menu.

TIP

Not only can you modify the size of the entire Exploring window (just like any other window), but you can also resize the panes within the Exploring window. To widen the Contents of pane and correspondingly narrow the All Folders pane, position the mouse pointer on the dividing line between the two and then drag to the left when the pointer changes to a double-headed arrow.

Note that, when resizing the panes of the Exploring window, Windows 95 automatically adds scroll bars to one or both of the panes if you make it too narrow to show all its goodies.

What do I do with it?

You can use the Explorer to open files (and their associated application programs), start programs, and move or copy files to different disks on your computer (or even to networked drives if you're on a network).

Opening files

You can open a file (and its associated program) with the Explorer by following just a couple of steps:

1. Open the file's folder in the All Folders pane.

2. Double-click the file's icon in the Contents of pane (or click the file's icon to select it and then choose the Open command on the file's context menu).

If Windows can identify the program that created this file and that program is not already open, it starts the program as part of opening the selected file. If Windows can't identify the program used to create the file, it opens the Open With dialog box, and you must choose the program to open the selected file from the programs shown in its list box.

TIP

If you're not sure whether the file you've located in the Contents of pane is really the one you want to open, try clicking the file icon with the secondary mouse button (usually the rightmost button for right-handers and leftmost button for lefties) to open the file's shortcut menu. If the file is of a type whose contents you can view prior to opening it (like a 1-2-3 or Excel worksheet or a Word document), you see a Quick View command near the top of the context menu. Select this command to open a Quick View window revealing the contents of the file.

If, after snooping around the file, you find that it is the one you want to open, choose the Open File for Editing command on the Quick View window's File pull-down menu or click the Open File for Editing button on the Quick View toolbar (it's the first one). If you find that the file isn't the one you want, you can close the Quick View window by either clicking its Close button or choosing the Exit command on its File menu. For more on snooping in files with this nifty little feature, *see* "Getting a Quick View of a File's Contents" in Part III.

Moving files

You can move a file to a new folder or a new disk in the Explorer by using either the drag-and-drop method or the cut-and-paste method. First, here are the steps for moving a file around in the Explorer with drag and drop:

1. In the All Folders pane, open the folder that contains the file you want to move and then click the file's icon in the Contents of pane to select it.

• If you want to move a bunch of files that are all next to each other, select them as a unit by positioning the mouse pointer

above and slightly to the left of the file icon in the upper-left corner and then drag down on a diagonal to draw a bounding box that includes all the other files to be moved.

- You can select a group of individual, non-adjacent files in the folder by holding down the Ctrl key as you click each one.

2. Use the vertical scroll bar in the All Folders pane to bring the icon for the destination disk or folder (where you want the file or files you've selected to move to) into view in the All Folders pane of the Exploring window.

3. Drag the icon(s) for the file(s) selected in the Contents of pane to the destination folder or disk icon in the All Folders pane.

As you drag the file icon(s), you see a ghosted version of the file(s) fly across the border from one pane to the other.

4. When the name of the destination disk or folder is highlighted, release the mouse button to move the file(s).

Remember: Windows automatically *moves* files when you drag their file icons from one folder to another on the same disk and *copies* files (indicated by the appearance of a plus sign next to the pointer) when you drag their icons from one disk to another.

Drag-and-drop moving from folder to folder is great because it's really fast. However, this method does have a major drawback in that it is pretty easy to think that you're dropping your little file icons into one folder when in fact you're dropping them into another, nearby folder. And what an awful surprise when you open up what you thought was the destination folder only to find that your files are gone. (If this happens to you, don't panic; you can locate them by using the Find Files or Folders command. *See* "Finding Files and Folders" in Part III.)

If you want to avoid the possibility of dropping your files in the wrong folder, you can use the somewhat clunkier but more foolproof cut-and-paste method to move your files in the Explorer by following these steps:

1. In the All Folders pane of the Exploring window, open the folder that contains the file(s) you want to move and then select the icon(s) for the file(s) in the Contents of pane.

2. Choose the Cut command from the Edit pull-down menu of the Exploring window or press Ctrl+X to move the selected file(s) to the Clipboard.

3. In the All Folders pane, open the destination folder (where you want the selected file or files to move to).

4. Choose the Paste command from the Edit pull-down menu of the Exploring window or press Ctrl+V to insert the file(s) into the folder which is open in the Contents of pane.

Copying files

Copying files from one folder to another or from one disk to another in the Explorer requires only the slightest variation of the technique for moving files described previously, regardless of whether you opt for the drag-and-drop or the cut-and-paste method.

✦ To *copy* — rather than *move* — files from one folder to another on the same disk with drag and drop, you just have to remember to hold down the Ctrl key as you drag your file icons to the destination folder. Of course, you don't have to do anything special to copy files when you're dragging their icons from a folder on one disk to a folder on another disk — for example, copying a file from hard drive C to floppy drive A or to a networked drive called Hd or Albert (drive E).

✦ To copy files from one folder to another (whether or not they're on the same disk), you only have to remember to choose Copy on the Edit pull-down menu or press Ctrl+C (rather than choosing Cut on the Edit menu or pressing Ctrl+X). The rest of the steps for copying are the same as those for moving with cut and paste.

If all you want to do is back up some files from your hard disk to a floppy disk in drive A or B, after selecting the files to copy, just open the context menu attached to one of the file icons and then select the correct floppy drive such as $5^1/_4$ Floppy (A) or (B), or $3^1/_2$ Floppy (A) or (B) on the Send To continuation menu. Oh, and one thing more: Don't forget to insert a floppy disk, preferably already formatted and ready to go, before you start this little operation.

Displaying the toolbar in the Exploring window

The Toolbar command on the View menu in the Exploring window turns on and off the display of a toolbar at the top of this window. Among other things, this toolbar makes it really easy to select the resources you want displayed in the Contents of pane and change the way the folder and file icons in this pane are shown.

✦ Use the Go to a different folder drop-down list box on the toolbar to select the resource whose contents you want displayed in the Contents of pane below. Click 🔼 on the toolbar to move up one level in the org chart shown in the All Folders pane following.

✦ Use 🔏, 📋, and 📋 on the toolbar to move or copy files or folders.

✦ Use ↶ on the toolbar to undo your latest boo-boo.

✦ Use ✗ on the toolbar to get rid of the files or folders you've selected.

✦ Use 🖆 on the toolbar to get properties information about the disks, files, or folders you've selected.

✦ Click 🖳 on the toolbar to the change the objects shown in the Contents of pane from large to small icons.

✦ Click 🖳 to view the contents with small icons in a multicolumn layout.

✦ Click 🖳 to view the contents with small icons in a single column along with information such as size, type, and date last modified.

✦ Click 🖳 on the toolbar to once again view the contents with the regular big icons.

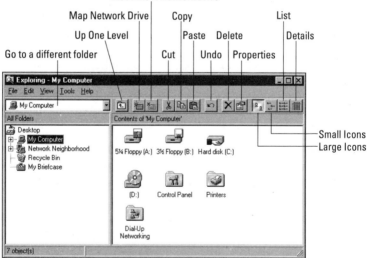

If you're using Windows 95 on a LAN (Local Area Network), you can click 🖳 on the toolbar to create a connection to a drive on somebody else's computer so that you can access the stuff on it (provided that you know how to designate or select the network path for that drive). Use 🖳 on the toolbar to break a connection with a particular network drive that is currently mapped onto your computer.

More stuff

Note that you can also use the My Computer icon at the top of the desktop to view the contents of your computer and do stuff like move and copy files. (*See* "My Computer" later in Part II, if you want to know more about this part of Windows 95).

See also "Moving Files and Folders," in Part III, for more stuff on moving files and folders.

See also "Copying Files and Folders," in Part III, for more on copying.

Files

Files contain all the precious data that you create with those sophisticated (and expensive) software programs based on Windows 95. Files occupy a certain amount of space (rated in K, or kilobytes, which is Greek for thousands of bytes) on a particular disk, be it your hard disk or a removable floppy disk.

The location of a file (known in Techese as the file's *pathname*) is identified by the letter of the drive that holds its disk, the folder or folders within which it's embedded (*see* "Folders" next in Part II), and a unique filename. (*See* "Long Filenames" later in Part II for a rundown on the name game.)

How do I get to it?

You can locate files on a disk in the Windows Explorer (*see* "Explorer" later in Part II) or the My Computer window (*see* "My Computer" later in Part II) or with the Find Files feature (*see* "Finding Files and Folders" in Part III).

If you need to edit or print a file on a routine basis and you want fast access to it (without having to remember which disk it's on and which folder it's in), create a shortcut for the file and locate the shortcut on the desktop (*see* "Shortcuts" later in Part II to learn how). That way, you can open the file by double-clicking its shortcut on the desktop, avoiding all that rigmarole of first having to locate the file with the Explorer or My Computer.

What do I do with it?

There's no end to the file activities in Windows 95; they can keep you occupied the whole day long.

✦ Open a file (and its associated program if that program is identifiable) by double-clicking its file icon.

+ Print a file (with the associated program) by dragging its file icon to a printer in the Printer folders or to a printer shortcut on the desktop.

+ Move or copy files between disks. (*See* "Copying Files and Folders" and "Moving Files and Folders" in Part III.)

+ Get rid of files (and free up the space they're taking up) when they are no longer of any use to you. (*See* "Deleting Junk" in Part III.)

Remember: You can get lots of good information on a file, like which program created it, how big it is, when it was created and last revised, and so on, by choosing the Properties command on the file's context menu. (*See* "Properties" later in Part II for details.)

More stuff

In Windows 95, files are assigned their own icons as well as their own filenames. Whenever possible, Windows 95 gives the file an icon identifying the program that created it. For example, the Excel worksheet icon features a sheet of paper with writing and Microsoft's XL logo, and the Word for Windows 95 icon features a sheet of paper with writing and a big blue W. When Windows 95 can't figure out exactly which program created the file, it assigns the file a generic file icon (which shows a blank sheet of paper with the standard Windows logo on it). For more on using file icons to identify the program that created them, *see* "Icons" later in Part II.

You can create an empty file that's associated with a particular program or type of program without having to open that program first. (*See* "Creating New Files and Folders" in Part III to find out how to do this.)

Folders

Folders are the data containers in Windows 95. They can contain files or other folders or a combination of files and folders. Like files, folders occupy a certain amount of space (rated in K, or kilobytes, and indicating the size of the data files it holds) on a particular disk, be it your hard disk or a removable floppy disk.

The location of a folder (known in Techese as the folder's *directory path*) is identified by the letter of the drive that holds its disk, the other folder or folders within which it's embedded, and a unique name. (*See* "Long Filenames" in Part II for a rundown on the name game.)

How do I get to it?

You can locate folders on a disk in the Windows Explorer (*see* "Explorer" earlier in Part II) or the My Computer window (*see* "My Computer" later in Part II) or with the Find Files feature (*see* "Finding Files and Folders" in Part III).

If you routinely work on a particular folder's files and you want fast access to them (without having to remember the folder's exact location on the disk), create a shortcut for the folder and place this shortcut on the desktop (*see* "Shortcuts" later in Part II to learn how). That way, you can open the folder and get to its files by double-clicking the folder's shortcut right on the desktop, avoiding all the bother of first having to locate the folder in the Explorer or My Computer.

What do I do with it?

There are lots of fun things you can do to folders in Windows 95:

✦ Open a folder and have a look at the files and other folders inside by double-clicking the parent folder icon.

✦ Move or copy a folder to a new location on its disk or to a new disk (*see* "Copying Files and Folders" and "Moving Files and Folders" in Part III).

✦ Delete the little darlings (and all the stuff they contain) when they are no longer needed (*see* "Deleting Junk" in Part III).

Remember: You can get lots of good information on a folder, like how many objects (folders and files) it contains, how big it is, and when it was created, by choosing the Properties command on the folder's context menu (*see* "Properties" later in Part II for details).

More stuff

In Windows 95, most folders use the generic (and boring) folder icon, meaning that the only thing unique about a folder is its pathname (its location on the disk and its name).

To learn how to create and name a new empty folder in Windows 95, *see* "Creating New Files and Folders" in Part III.

Icons

Icons are the small pictures identifying the type of object (be it a disk drive, folder, file, or some other such thing) that you're dealing with in Windows 95.

How do I get to it?

Everywhere you turn in Windows 95, you run into icons. They're all over on the desktop, and the My Computer and Exploring windows are lousy with them. In the following figure, you see a bunch of the different types of icons that you meet in the Contents of pane of the Exploring window when you go looking around in the Windows folder.

What do I do with it?

Most icons in Windows 95 are made for double-clicking. Double-clicking an icon does different stuff depending upon the type of icon it is. For example

+ If the icon represents a program or a shortcut to a program, double-clicking the icon starts the program.

+ If the icon represents a file or a shortcut to a file and Windows can recognize the program that created it, double-clicking its icon starts the program (if it's not already running) and opens the file. If Windows doesn't recognize the file's creator, it opens the Open With dialog box, where you choose a program to try to open the file.

+ If the icon represents a folder, double-clicking the icon opens the folder and displays the folder's contents.

TIP

If you can't tell from an icon's picture what the blazes it's for, you can always open its context menu and choose the Properties command. Doing this displays a *such 'n' such* Properties dialog box that gives you the lowdown on what type of object you're dealing with.

More stuff

Normally, Windows 95 gives you large icons in the windows that you open. If you want, you can modify the appearance of the icons as well as determine in what order they appear (a job that Windows 95 usually does all by itself). *See* "Arranging the Icons in a Window" and "Changing the View Options in a Window" in Part III for specific information.

Long Filenames

Long filenames in Windows 95 let you name your files and folders whatever the heck you want up to a maximum of 255 characters (including *spaces!*).

How do I get to it?

File and folder names are displayed beneath their icons when the Large Icons view option is used, and to the immediate right of their icons when any other viewing option is used (*see* "Changing the View Options in a Window" in Part III).

What do I do with it?

When you create a new file or folder with the New command on a window's File pull-down menu, Windows gives the file or folder a temporary file or folder name, like New Excel 5.0 Worksheet or New Folder. You can replace this temporary name with one of your own by typing your new name — the new name replaces the highlighted temporary name. If you don't care about the name at the time you create it, you can just accept it by pressing Enter or clicking the mouse somewhere outside its icon or name.

If you're creating a new file within an application running under Windows 95, you need to give that file a unique filename at the time you first save it (although many Windows programs do give you some kind of catchy temporary name — Document1 and the like).

Keep in mind that at any time you can rename any file, folder, or shortcut that you create in Windows (for some of the stuff created by Windows itself, this is not true). To rename a file or folder on the desktop or in a window, click on its name and then edit or replace the name. (*See* "Renaming Files and Folders," in Part III, for more on renaming files.)

Although Windows 95 and its new accessories, like WordPad (*see* "Accessories" earlier in Part II for details), support long filenames, many of the older programs and accessories that you will run under Windows 95 still do not. And as of this writing — when Windows 95 has just hit the market — many of the programs you're likely to use are in that "older" category. This means that if you create a new Excel 5.0 file in Windows 95 and then give it a long filename like

```
New Sleeping Beauty Product List
```

and then try to open this file with Excel 5.0, all you see of this lovely filename in Excel's Open dialog box is

```
newsleep.xls
```

The filename is so truncated because in programs created for previous versions of Windows, filenames for DOS and Windows programs like Excel and Word are limited to eight characters with no spaces. And that will be the case until you buy Microsoft's new Windows 95 versions of its spreadsheet and other programs. Worse yet, if you try double-clicking the Excel icon for the New Sleeping Beauty Product List file, Excel gives you a nasty error message when it opens, indicating that it can't find a file named

```
C:\EXCEL\New Sleeping Beauty Product List.xls
```

This means that you have to cool it with the long filenames when using software programs designed for pre-95 versions of Windows (3.1 and 3.11), or else you'll have to open each file within the application and see your long filenames reduced to mangled and unintelligible eight-dot-three filenames (the "three" being a three-character filename extension usually supplied by the program itself to identify its file type — like .xls for eXceL workSheet).

This situation can get even worse: Go ahead and put your files with the long filenames in folders with long folder names. Then try to get at them with a pre-Windows 95 application. For example, say I create a new, empty Word file named

```
Mr. Handley's Spring 95 Performance Review
```

in a folder named

```
Greg's Worksheets
```

To open this document within Word 6.0, I have to find the

```
mrhandle.doc
```

in the

```
greg'swo
```

directory on my hard disk! Given how badly Word mangled my long file and folder names, I would be better off observing the eight-dot-three file-naming convention when I create names in Windows 95 (even though I don't have to) and coming up with my own abbreviations, like

```
hndperfm.doc
```

in the folder named

```
gregxls
```

Although there's nothing pretty about these file and folder names, at least they convey the gist of their contents to me, if for no other reason than I had to wrack my poor brain to come up with the abbreviations.

More stuff

Windows 95 normally hides the DOS filename extensions for the file types that it recognizes. If you want to see these filename extensions in the Explorer and the My Computer window, you need to choose the Options command from the View pull-down menu in one of these windows. Then select the Hide MS-DOS file extensions for file types that are registered check box to remove its check mark.

Microsoft Exchange

The Microsoft Exchange lets you send messages, e-mail, and faxes to computers that are either networked to yours or have access via a modem to a fax machine or an on-line service like the Microsoft Network.

How do I get to it?

The Inbox icon for the Microsoft Exchange is one of the icons found right on the desktop (provided that you installed the Microsoft Exchange when installing Windows 95). To open the Inbox-Microsoft Exchange window showing the folders in the Microsoft Exchange, double-click the Inbox icon.

What do I do with it?

When you double-click the Inbox Microsoft Exchange icon, Windows 95 either

+ displays a Log On dialog box that prompts you to either accept the default start-up profile (which is the one you selected for use when starting the Microsoft Exchange when setting up the profiles with the Microsoft Exchange Profiles control panel) or to select another profile to use

or

+ just opens the Microsoft Exchange window using your computer's default profile

Which of the two Windows 95 does is determined by whether your system administrator has selected the Pick the profile that will be used or the Always use which profile radio button in the When starting Microsoft Exchange section on the General tab of the Microsoft Exchange options dialog box.

If you get the Choose Profile dialog box when you double-click the Inbox icon, to select a new messaging profile, choose its name in the Profile Name drop-down list box in the Log On dialog box.

If you want to make one of the profiles in this drop-down list the new default start-up profile, select the Options>> button near the bottom of the Log On dialog box. Choosing this button expands the dialog box to include a Set as Default Profile and Show Log On Screen for all Information Services check boxes. To make the message profile shown in the Profile Name edit box the default, select the Set as Default Profile check box before you choose the OK button to start the Microsoft Exchange.

After you select the messaging profile to use (or just double-click), Windows opens a window appropriate to the profile you selected.

✦ If you choose a messaging profile that includes getting on-line with the Microsoft Network, Windows opens the Sign In dialog box where you can connect with the Microsoft Network.

✦ If you choose a profile for using Microsoft Mail, Windows opens an Exploring window with the Personal Information Store, which includes folders for the Deleted Items, Inbox, Outbox, and Sent Items.

✦ If you choose a profile for using the Microsoft Fax service to send and receive faxes with your modem, Windows opens this same Exploring window after initializing your modem (which needs to be connected to your telephone line, turned on, and ready to go).

If you select the Show Log On Screens for all Information Services check box in the Options section of the Choose Profile dialog box, Windows 95 opens one or more of the following dialog boxes (depending upon what messaging services are included in the profile) as part of opening the Microsoft Exchange:

✦ **Settings for the Microsoft Network:** This dialog box enables you to make changes to the settings for the entire network.

✦ **Personal Address Book:** This dialog box enables you to select a new address book or change the order in which names appear in the personal address book.

✦ **Microsoft Personal Information Store:** This dialog box enables you to change the password for using the store or compress the store file to make it smaller.

✦ **Microsoft Mail:** This dialog box enables you to change all sorts of settings related to your post office and how you get your e-mail.

✦ **Microsoft Fax Properties:** This dialog box enables you to set all sorts of things related to faxing, such as what type of cover page (if any) to use, what modem to use, and a whole bunch of information about you and your location in the company.

Sending messages

To send a message to your buddies on the LAN (Local Area Network) or to send an e-mail to someone on the Microsoft Network from the Exploring window for the Microsoft Exchange, follow these steps:

1. Start the Microsoft Exchange with a profile that uses the Microsoft Mail, CompuServe Mail, or MS Internet Mail Service messaging service (*see* the preceding "What do I do with it?" section for information on selecting a new profile when you start the Microsoft Exchange).

2. Choose New Message on the Compose pull-down menu in the Exploring - Microsoft Exchange window (or press Ctrl+N) to open the Microsoft Exchange window that has blank To, Cc, and Subject edit boxes followed by a big blank list box, where you can enter your message.

3. Type the names of the message's recipients in the To edit box, each separated by a semicolon.

TIP

You can also click the To button to open the Select Names dialog box, where you can designate the recipients' names by selecting them in the left-hand list box and then clicking the To-> button to copy their names (separated by semicolons) to the upper right-hand Message Recipients list box.

You can select a new list to use by choosing it in the Show Names drop-down list box and designate the people to be copied on the message by selecting their names in the left-hand list box and then clicking the Cc-> button to copy them to the lower right-hand Message Recipients list box. When you finish selecting the recipients' names, choose OK or press Enter.

4. Type the name of the people to be copied on the message in the Cc edit box (if you didn't already select them in the Select Names dialog box described in Step 3). Be sure to separate each person's name with a semicolon in the Cc edit box.

If you prefer, you can reopen the Select Names dialog box by clicking the Cc button to the immediate left of this text box. Once this dialog box is open, you can choose the folks that are to be copied on the message by selecting their names in the left-hand list box and then clicking the Cc-> button to copy them to the lower right-hand list box.

5. Type the subject of the message, if appropriate, in the Subject edit box.

6. Type the body of the message in the large, blank list box right below the Subject edit box.

TIP

When you select this area, the second toolbar (with the Font, Font Size, and other formatting buttons) becomes active, enabling you to change fonts, add attributes such as bold, italics, and underlining, add bullet points, and switch between left, center, and right justification of the text. When typing the text of the message, press Enter to terminate paragraphs or insert blank lines and press Tab to indent a line.

If you wish, you can insert the contents of files or other messages (perhaps the one that your message is answering) or objects (like charts or other types of graphics) into the message.

- To insert a file, choose File on the Insert pull-down menu.

- To insert a message, choose Message on the Insert menu.

- To insert a graphic of some kind, choose Object on the Insert menu.

When inserting a file or message, you can choose between inserting its contents as text only or as an attachment to your message. When inserting a graphic of some kind, you can choose between creating a new graphic (with the same tools found in the Paint accessory) or creating it from an existing graphics file.

7. When you're finished composing the message, you can send it to all the recipients shown in the To and Cc edit boxes by choosing Send on the File menu, clicking the Send button on the top toolbar (it's the very first button on the left), or pressing Ctrl+Enter.

You can add a From edit box and/or a Bcc edit box to the other boxes automatically attached to the new message you're composing in the Microsoft Exchange. To do this, choose the From Box or Bcc Box command on the View pull-down menu of the Microsoft Exchange window.

✦ To add the sender's name to the From edit box, either type the appropriate name there (your name, unless you are sending a message for someone else) or click the From button and select the name in the Select Names dialog box.

✦ To add the names to the <u>B</u>cc edit box to send a "blind" copy, type the names, separated by semicolons, or click the <u>B</u>cc button and then select the names in the Select Names dialog box.

You can also use <u>N</u>ew Message on the Co<u>m</u>pose pull-down menu (or press Ctrl+N) in Microsoft Exchange to send a fax. This lets you insert files and other stuff like graphics and format the message text before sending your fax. Simply follow the preceding instructions for composing a message. After you finish your message

1. Choose Fax <u>A</u>ddressing Wizard in the <u>T</u>ools pull-down menu. The Fax Addressing Wizard opens with the recipient of your message selected.

2. Type the fax number of your recipient in the <u>F</u>ax # edit boxes.

3. Press Finish to return to the Compose Message window.

To send your fax, do one of the following:

✦ Click the Send button on the menu bar.

✦ Choose Se<u>n</u>d from the <u>F</u>ile pull-down menu.

✦ Press Ctrl+Enter.

Sending faxes

To send a fax with a fax/modem connected to your computer from the Microsoft Exchange with the Compose New Fax Wizard, follow these steps:

1. Start the Microsoft Exchange with a profile that uses the Microsoft Fax messaging service (*see* the preceding "What do I do with it?" section for information on selecting a new profile when you start the Microsoft Exchange).

2. Choose Ne<u>w</u> Fax on the Co<u>m</u>pose pull-down menu of the Microsoft Exchange window to open the Compose New Fax Wizard dialog box.

3. Click the Next> button and type the name of the fax recipient in the <u>N</u>ame edit box. Next, type the fax number of your recipient and check the <u>D</u>ial area code box if you are calling to an area code other than your own. If the fax number you're dialing doesn't require a long distance country code (such as 1 for the U.S.), be sure that you choose the (None - internal extension) option in the C<u>o</u>untry code drop-down list box.

4. Follow the prompts on the next few pages of the Compose New Fax Wizard, indicating who, where, and how to send the fax.

5. When you arrive at the last page, choose the Finish button to send your fax.

More stuff

See also "Microsoft Exchange Profiles," in Part V, for information on setting up a new profile for the Microsoft Exchange.

See also "Modems," in Part V, for information on installing a fax/modem.

See also "Fax," in Part IV, for more information on using the Compose New Fax Wizard, creating a new fax cover page, or retrieving a document from a remote fax service.

The Microsoft Network

The Microsoft Network is an on-line service through which you can exchange e-mail with your cohorts, give 'em your two cents on various chat forums, and even get onto the much ballyhooed Internet! (Unfortunately, this great on-line service cannot be accessed with the Preview version of Windows 95.)

How do I get to it?

To set up an account for using The Microsoft Network, follow these steps:

1. Double-click The Microsoft Network icon on the desktop to open The Microsoft Network window, where you can sign up or log on to the Network.

2. Choose OK or press Enter to go on to the second screen of The Microsoft Network window.

3. Enter your area code and the first three digits of your telephone number in the appropriate edit boxes on the second screen of The Microsoft Network window and then choose OK or press Enter.

4. Choose the Connect button or press Enter to dial up The Microsoft Network and follow the prompts to set up an account with your member ID and password.

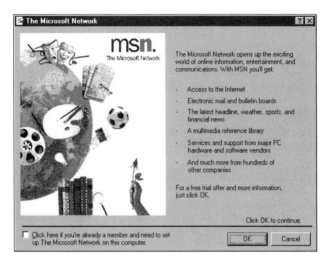

After signing up for The Microsoft Network, you can log on to the network by following these steps:

1. Double-click the MSN Microsoft Network icon on the desktop to open The Microsoft Network window (shown in the preceding figure).

2. Click the Click here if you're already a member and need to set up The Microsoft Network on this computer check box and then choose OK or press Enter.

3. Windows 95 opens the Sign In dialog box for The Microsoft Network, where you enter your Member ID and Password (if the Remember my password check box is not selected).

4. Choose the Connect button to go on-line on The Microsoft Network.

What do I do with it?

The Microsoft Network lets you send and receive e-mail from friends and business associates that have Windows 95 and are signed up for this service. You can also participate in various discussion forums and get on-line help and advice for any problems you may encounter with any Windows software you're running (including Windows 95).

At some point in its development, The Microsoft Network is also supposed to offer access to various on-line news services as well as to the almighty Internet.

More stuff

See also "Mail and Fax," in Part V, for information on setting up profiles for using The Microsoft Network Online Service.

See also "Modems," in Part V, for information on installing a fax/modem for connecting to The Microsoft Network.

My Briefcase

My Briefcase lets you synchronize versions of files from different computers or disks so that you don't drive yourself crazy trying to figure out which version of the file isn't as up-to-date as the other one.

How do I get to it?

The My Briefcase icon is found right on the desktop (provided that you installed this utility when installing Windows 95). To open the My Briefcase window, simply double-click the My Briefcase icon.

What do I do with it?

To use My Briefcase to synchronize versions of a file, you must copy the original file to the Briefcase on the desktop as follows:

1. Use the Explorer or My Computer to locate and open the folder containing the files that you want to keep up to date.

2. Drag the files' icons to the My Briefcase icon.

When you release the mouse button, Windows 95 copies the selected files into the Briefcase.

After you copy the original files to My Briefcase, you can then take these copies of the files with you by moving My Briefcase to another diskette or another computer (like a laptop connected to your desktop computer with the Direct Cable Connection accessory). To move My Briefcase, you follow these steps:

1. Use the Explorer or My Computer to open the disk (such as a diskette in drive A or the hard disk of a laptop computer connected to your desktop computer).

2. Drag the My Briefcase icon to the icon for the disk drive with diskette or hard disk on a connected computer in the Exploring or My Computer window.

When you release the mouse button, Windows 95 moves My Briefcase (as well as the copies of the files it contains) to the designated diskette or hard disk drive.

Synchronizing files

After moving My Briefcase to a diskette or a hard disk on another computer, you can make changes to it as you see fit. If you then need to check these files against their original versions on the original computer, you can do so by moving My Briefcase back to the original computer as follows:

1. Place the diskette with My Briefcase in the disk drive of the original computer or connect the laptop computer whose hard disk contains My Briefcase to the original computer.

2. Display the My Briefcase icon that contains the files that need synchronizing in the Exploring or My Computer window.

3. Drag the My Briefcase icon from the diskette or the hard disk of the laptop computer to the desktop of the original computer.

4. Double-click the My Briefcase icon to open the My Briefcase window.

5. If necessary, open the View pull-down menu in this window and select the Details command so that you can see all the file details (including the updating status) for the files shown in the My Briefcase window.

6. If some of the files in My Briefcase need updating in regard to the originals on the desktop computer, the message Needs Updating appears in the Status column.

- To update all files that need updating, choose the Update <u>A</u>ll command on the <u>B</u>riefcase pull-down menu.

- To update only particular files that need updating, select them in the list box and then choose the <u>U</u>pdate Selection command on the <u>B</u>riefcase menu instead.

When you choose Update <u>A</u>ll or <u>U</u>pdate Selection, Windows 95 opens the Update My Briefcase dialog box, which shows which version of each set of files will be replaced.

7. Normally, Windows replaces the earlier versions of the files shown in the Update My Briefcase dialog box with later versions. To change this order for a particular set of files, click the file in the set that should replace the other with the secondary mouse button to open its shortcut menu and then select the Replace command on the menu that has the arrow pointing away from that file toward the version it is to replace.

8. To skip any replacing for a particular set of files, choose the Skip command on one of the file's shortcut menus.

9. When you have all the replacements properly figured out, choose the Update button at the bottom of the Update My Briefcase dialog box or press Enter.

In this figure, you see the My Briefcase window when a single file named Briefdoc requires updating.

When you choose the Update <u>A</u>ll or <u>U</u>pdate Selection commands on the <u>B</u>riefcase menu, Windows displays an Update My Briefcase dialog box similar to the one that follows:

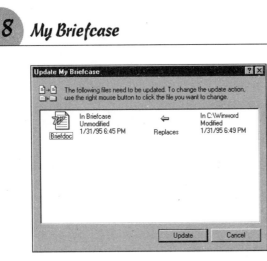

In this figure, you see the prompt for replacing a slightly earlier (unmodified) version of Briefdoc in My Briefcase with the later (modified) version of Briefdoc in the Winword folder on the hard disk. To replace the later (modified) version in the Winword folder with the earlier (unmodified) version in My Briefcase, follow these steps:

1. Click the text In Briefcase Unmodified 1/31/95 6:45 PM following the Briefdoc file icon with the secondary mouse button.

2. Choose the Replace command that shows an arrow pointing to the text In C:\Winword Modified 1/31/95 6:49 PM.

3. Choose the Update button.

Creating a briefcase

So what do you do if you don't have a My Briefcase icon on your desktop in the first place? Well, you can create one by following these steps:

1. Click the desktop with the secondary mouse button to open its context menu.

2. Choose New on the desktop context menu to open its continuation menu.

3. Choose Briefcase from the New continuation menu to add an icon called New Briefcase to the desktop.

4. To rename the icon called New Briefcase to "My Briefcase," "Rose's Briefcase," or whatever you want it known by, click the icon's filename. Once it's selected, type the new name and press Enter.

Don't create more than one Briefcase to hold the files you want to keep synchronized. After creating My Briefcase, just keep moving its icon from computer to computer (either via diskette or direct cable connection) and using its update commands to keep the versions of your files properly synchronized.

More stuff

If you ever decide that you no longer care about synchronizing a particular file in your Briefcase with its original, you can break the link between the files. Here's how:

1. Open the My Briefcase window.

2. Select that file in this list box.

3. Choose the Split From Original command on the Briefcase pull-down menu.

4. A warning dialog box appears and asks whether you are sure that you want to prevent any further updates of the file you've selected. To go ahead and split the Briefcase file from its original, choose the Yes button or press Enter in this dialog box.

After choosing the Yes button, Windows considers the file to be an orphan (don't tell Newt) and will no longer prompt you to update it regardless of what changes you make to its contents or how long the file is located in the Briefcase.

See also "Explorer," earlier in Part II, for information on locating files and folders with the Explorer.

See also "My Computer," later in Part II, for information on locating files and folders with My Computer.

See also "Finding Files and Folders," in Part III, for more information on finding files with the Find command on the Start menu.

See also "Copying Files and Folders," in Part III, for more information on copying files.

See also "Moving Files and Folders," in Part III, for more information on moving files.

See also "Direct Cable Connection," in Part IV, for information on connecting two computers together with the Direct Cable Connection accessory.

My Computer

My Computer gives you quick access to all the major parts of your computer, including the hard disk, floppy, CD-ROM, and networked drives, fonts, Control Panel, printers, and dial-up networking.

How do I get to it?

My Computer is one of the few permanent desktop icons in Windows 95. To open the My Computer window and have a look-see at your computer system, just double-click the My Computer icon in the very upper-left corner of the desktop.

What do I do with it?

The My Computer window is most useful for getting a quick look-see at the contents of parts of your computer. To see what's on a drive or to open one of the folders in the My Computer window, simply double-click an icon as follows:

+ If you double-click a drive icon, such as $3^1/_2$ Floppy (A:) or Hard disk (C:), Windows 95 opens a new window showing the folders and files on that disk.

+ If you double-click a floppy drive that doesn't have a disk in it, Windows 95 gives you an error message indicating that the drive is not ready. If you meant to put a floppy in the drive, do so and then click the Retry button or press Enter.

+ If the disk in the floppy drive is not formatted, Windows displays an alert box asking you whether you want to format the disk now. To format the disk, choose the Yes button or press Enter to open the Format dialog box (*see* "Formatting a Disk" in Part III).

✦ If you double-click a CD-ROM drive icon and the drive contains an audio CD, Windows opens the CD Player and starts playing the compact disc (*see* "Playing CDs" in Part III for details). If the drive contains a cool game or some other data disk, Windows just opens a standard window showing the stuff on the CD-ROM (in the case of a game that you've never played, double-click the Install icon).

✦ If you double-click the Control Panel icon, Windows opens the Control Panel window with all the familiar Control Panel utility icons (*see* "Control Panel" earlier in Part II).

✦ If you double-click the Printers folder icon, Windows opens the Printers window showing all the printers currently installed on your system (*see* "Printers" under "Control Panel" earlier in Part II).

✦ If you double-click the Dial-Up Networking icon, Windows opens the Dial-Up Networking window showing all the dial-up connections that you've created on your system or the Welcome to Dial-Up Networking Wizard if you've never created any dial-up connections (*see* "Dial-Up Networking" in Part IV).

If you don't want Windows to open a separate window each time you double-click an icon in the My Computer window but would instead prefer to have Windows just replace the My Computer window with the one you're opening, choose Options from the View pull-down menu and then select the Browse folders by using a single window that changes as you open each folder radio button on the Folder tab.

Displaying the toolbar in the My Computer window

The Toolbar command on the View menu in the My Computer window turns on and off the display of a toolbar at the top of this window. Among other things, this toolbar makes it really easy to select the object you want to view and change the way its contents are shown in the window.

✦ Use the Go to a different folder drop-down list box on the toolbar to select the object whose contents you want displayed in the list box below. Click [🗁] on the toolbar to move up one level in the list shown in the drop-down menu.

✦ Use [✂], [🗎], and [📋] on the toolbar to move or copy files or folders.

✦ Use [↺] on the toolbar to undo your latest boo-boo.

✦ Use [✗] on the toolbar to get rid of the files or folders you've selected.

♦ Use 🖼 on the toolbar to get properties information about the disks, files, or folders you've selected.

♦ Click ⬝⬝ on the toolbar to change the objects shown in the list box from large to small icons.

♦ Click ⬝⬝⬝ to view the contents shown in the list box with small icons in a multicolumn layout.

♦ Click ▦ to view the contents shown in the list box with small icons in a single column along with information like size, type, and date last modified.

♦ Click ᴅᴅ on the toolbar to once again view the contents shown in the list box with the regular large icons.

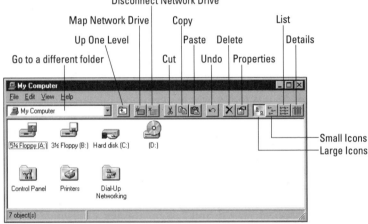

Disconnect Network Drive
Map Network Drive | Copy | List
Up One Level | Paste | Delete | Details
Go to a different folder | Cut | Undo | Properties
Small Icons
Large Icons

If you're using Windows 95 on a LAN (Local Area Network), you can click 🖼 on the toolbar to create a connection to a drive on somebody else's computer so that you can access the stuff on it (provided that you know how to designate or select the network path for that drive). Use 🖼 on the toolbar to break a connection with a particular network drive that is currently mapped onto your computer.

More stuff

See also "Explorer," earlier in Part II, for alternative methods for displaying the contents of a disk and moving or copying files.

Network Neighborhood

The Network Neighborhood gives you an overview of all the workgroups, computers, and shared resources on your LAN (Local Area Network).

How do I get to it?

The Network Neighborhood is one of the few permanent desktop icons in Windows 95 (even if your computer is not networked to others at the time you install Windows — hey, you never know when you might just need to set up a Local Area Network of your own).

To open the Network Neighborhood window and have a look-see at your LAN, just double-click the Network Neighborhood icon.

What do I do with it?

The primary purpose of the Network Neighborhood is to give you a graphic view of the workgroups set up on your network and the resources that are networked together. When you open the Network Neighborhood window, Windows shows you the icons representing the entire network as well as each workgroup that you've established.

+ To see which computers and printers are part of your workgroup, double-click its icon.

+ To see all the workgroups and printers that are networked together, period, double-click the Entire Network icon.

More stuff

See also "Network," in Part V, for information on how to administrate your network with the Network control panel.

Properties

Each object represented by an icon in Windows 95 has its own set of properties that describe its current settings.

How do I get to it?

To open the *such 'n' such* Properties dialog box for a particular object and get the lowdown on its place in Windows 95, click the object's icon with the secondary mouse button (that's the one you don't normally click) to open its context menu (*see* "Context Menus" earlier in Part II) and select the Properties command on this menu.

The following figure shows the System Properties dialog box opened by selecting the Properties command on the My Computer context menu.

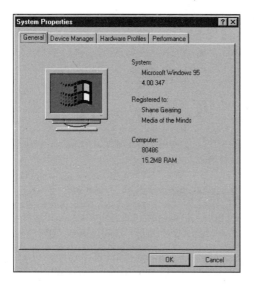

What do I do with it?

Most of the time, there's not much you can or want to do with the properties for a particular Windows object. Depending upon the object, you may have zero chance to change any of its settings. In those situations where Windows 95 does let you fool around with the property settings, please be very careful not to screw up your computer by foolishly selecting some incompatible setting that you had no business changing.

That said, you can safely play with a couple of cosmetic properties to your heart's content:

✦ To change the background pattern, choose a new wallpaper for the desktop, or select or change the screen saver for your monitor: Click anywhere on the desktop with the secondary mouse button and select the Properties command to open the Display Properties dialog box.

✦ To change when and how the taskbar appears on the desktop from the Start menu, clear all the files listed on the Documents continuation menu, or add or remove shortcuts or folders from the Programs continuation menu: Click anywhere on the taskbar with the secondary mouse button and select the Properties command to open the Taskbar Properties dialog box (*see* "Start Menu" and "Taskbar" later in Part II).

One of the more useful uses for the Properties command is getting the lowdown on how much free space is left on a disk. To get a reading on a disk

1. Click its drive icon with the secondary mouse button.

2. Select Properties on its context menu.

When Windows 95 opens the Hard disk (C:) or $3^{1}/_{2}$ Floppy (A:) Properties dialog box, you see the General tab showing the amount of Used and Free space in MB (megabytes) or K (kilobytes). You also see a nice pie chart at the bottom with two slices: one representing the free space and the other representing the used space. Note that when working with floppy disks, you can change the disk's volume label by editing or replacing the name displayed in the Label edit box at the top of the General tab.

More stuff

For more on properties in Windows, see *Windows 95 For Dummies,* Chapter 12.

Pull-Down Menus

Pull-down menus are the primary means for making your wishes known in Windows 95. Although you'd think by their name that the commands on pull-down menus would always appear below the menu, in some cases (like the Start menu), their options actually appear above the menu name when you open them.

How do I get to it?

Pull-down menus are found right below the title bar in all the windows and a very few of the dialog boxes that you open. To open a pull-down menu in the window or dialog box that's currently selected (the one whose title bar is highlighted), you have a few choices:

- ✦ Click the menu name on the menu bar.

- ✦ Hold down the Alt key as you type the command letter in the menu name (that is, the underlined letter).

- ✦ Press the F10 key to activate the menu bar and then either type the command letter in the menu name or press the ↓ or → key until the menu you want is highlighted. Then press the ↓ key to open the menu.

What do I do with it?

After you've got the pull-down menu open so you can see all the menu items, you are ready to choose one of its commands:

- ✦ Drag down (or up, in some rare cases) until the menu command is highlighted and then click the menu item (if you drag by just rolling over the menu items) or release the primary mouse button (if you drag by holding down the mouse button).

- ✦ Type the command letter of the menu item.

- ✦ Press the ↓ or ↑ key until the menu item is highlighted and then press the Enter key to select it.

Remember: Menu commands on a pull-down menu that have three dots (...) following the name open a dialog box of further choices when selected. Menu commands that have a right-pointing arrowhead following the name open a continuation menu with further choices when selected.

For pre-Windows 95 users only

Windows 95 introduces a much less stressful technique for dragging through the items in a pull-down menu that is totally unknown in earlier versions of Windows: You can now highlight menu items on an open pull-down menu simply by rolling the mouse pointer over the menu items with *no mouse buttons pressed!* That's right; instead of getting those awful hand cramps from having to hold the button down, just click to open the menu and then, with no further mouse button manipulation, "drag" through the items on a pull-down menu. You highlight the menu's items by rolling the mouse pointer over them.

Also, once you've opened one pull-down menu in a window, you can then open the other ones on the menu bar simply by rolling over the menu name (with no mouse button down). Likewise, you can open all continuation menus attached to a menu item simply by resting the mouse pointer on that item for a second (without clicking the item or holding the mouse button down).This new pull-down menu selection technique is universal in Windows 95, so you can use it on any pull-down menu in any program that runs under the new version of Windows (even when it's not been upgraded in any way for Windows 95).

When dragging through the items in a pull-down menu with no mouse button down, you select the menu item you want to choose by clicking the desired item after it's highlighted. This method is almost the direct opposite of one of the old ways of selecting such items, where you drag through the menu, mouse button pressed, until you reach (and thereby highlight) the desired item, at which point you release the mouse button (a method that still works in Windows 95, by the way).

More stuff

If you open the wrong pull-down menu in a window, press the Esc key to close the menu. You can then select another menu either with the arrow keys or by typing its command letter. If you want to bail out of the menus altogether, press Esc a second time to deactivate the pull-down menu bar.

See also "Context Menus" and "Dialog Boxes," earlier in Part II, for more on selecting commands in Windows 95.

Recycle Bin

The Recycle Bin is the trash can for Windows 95. Anything you delete in Windows goes into the Recycle Bin and stays there until you either retrieve the deleted item or empty the Recycle Bin.

How do I get to it?

The Recycle Bin icon is one of the few that stay on the desktop at all times. To open the Recycle Bin and take a gander at all the stuff you put into it or to rescue something from utter annihilation, double-click this icon to open the Recycle Bin dialog box.

Name	Original Location	Date Deleted	Type
Another Explorer	C:\WINDOWS\Profil...	12/22/94 1:27 PM	Shortcut
ANSISORT.GLB	C:\Post Office\Shan...	12/19/94 2:56 PM	GLB File
ANSISORT.GLB	C:\Lunkheads\wgpo...	12/19/94 3:12 PM	GLB File
ANSISORT.GLB	C:\Lunkheads\wgpo...	12/19/94 3:12 PM	GLB File
APPLET	C:\IDG\Win95	12/15/94 11:34 AM	Bitmap Picture Image
APPLET1	C:\IDG\Win95	12/21/94 2:30 PM	Bitmap Picture Image
Briefcase Database	C:\WINDOWS\Profil...	12/23/94 2:47 PM	File

325 object(s)   202KB

What do I do with it?

To fill the Recycle Bin with stuff you don't need anymore, do this:

1. Select the folders or files you no longer need.

2. Drag their icons to the Recycle Bin icon on the desktop and drop them in, press the Del key or, if you're in a window, choose Delete on the window's File pull-down menu.

To rescue stuff from the Recycle Bin, follow these steps:

1. Open the Recycle Bin dialog box by double-clicking the Recycle Bin icon on the desktop.

2. Select the icons for the files and folders you want to save from destruction.

3. Drag the selected folder and file icons out of the Recycle Bin dialog box and drop them either onto the desktop or into the folder where they belong, or choose Restore from the File pull-down menu to restore them to their rightful place.

To empty the Recycle Bin and permanently get rid of the stuff that's in it, do this:

1. Open the Recycle Bin dialog box by double-clicking the Recycle Bin icon on the desktop.

2. Choose Empty Recycle Bin from the File pull-down menu.

More stuff

The stuff that you get rid of by using the Del key or the Delete command on the File menu, or by dragging into the Recycle Bin, isn't gone until you choose the Empty Recycle Bin command from the File pull-down menu in the Recycle Bin dialog box. However, keep in mind that choosing this command immediately blows away everything in this dialog box, and like that old nursery rhyme says, "All the King's horses and all the King's men couldn't put the contents of the Recycle

Bin back together again!" In other words, don't ever empty the Recycle Bin until you've examined its contents and are absolutely sure that you'll never need to use any of those items ever again.

See also "Deleting Junk," in Part III, for more on getting rid of things in Windows 95.

Shortcuts

Shortcuts make it possible to open an object like a favorite document, folder, or program directly from the desktop of the computer even when you have absolutely no idea where this object is on your computer (giving you full usage of the important stuff on your computer while remaining blissfully ignorant of the stuff's whereabouts).

How do I get to it?

Although shortcuts can be located within a particular folder, most of the time you want to locate the shortcuts you create right out in the open on the desktop so that you can get right at them (it kinda defeats the purpose of shortcuts to hide them away in folders that you must locate and then open before you can use the shortcuts!).

Each time you create a shortcut for an object, Windows creates an icon for it with a name like Shortcut to *such and such* (unless a shortcut for that object already exists, in which case it would be called Another Shortcut to *such and such*). You can, of course, rename the shortcut to whatever name suits you, just as you can rename any file or folder in Windows (***see*** "Renaming Files and Folders" in Part III).

You can always tell a shortcut icon from the regular icon for a file, folder, printer, or program (even should you give the shortcut the same name as the object to which it refers — something I tend to do all the time) because the shortcut icon contains a little box with a curved arrow pointing up to the right like this Explorer shortcut.

What do I do with it?

To use a shortcut for a file, folder, or program, you double-click its shortcut icon to open the file, open the folder, or start the program. In the case of a shortcut for a printer, you can print a document with that printer by dragging the file's icon onto the shortcut icon.

To create a shortcut for an object in Windows 95, follow these steps:

1. Open the folder that contains the object (like a file, folder, printer, or program) you want to create a shortcut for.

2. Select the object's icon in the window.

3. Choose the Create Shortcut command on the File pull-down menu or on the object's context menu.

4. If Windows beeps at you and displays the error message Unable to create a shortcut here. Do you want the shortcut placed on the desktop?, choose Yes. If Windows doesn't give you this error message, it put the new shortcut in the currently open window. If you want the shortcut on the desktop where you have constant access to it, drag its icon to any place on the desktop and release the mouse button.

5. To rename the new shortcut, click somewhere in its temporary name to select just its text; then type the new shortcut name and press Enter.

You'll mess up a shortcut if you move the object to which it refers to a new place on your computer because Windows will still look for it (unsuccessfully) in the old location. If you do mess up a shortcut by moving the object it refers to, you have to trash the shortcut and then re-create it all over again or move the original file back to its location.

More stuff

One of the first shortcuts you should create (even before you create a shortcut to Minesweeper and Hearts) is a shortcut to the Windows Explorer so that you don't have to go through the trouble of clicking the Start button, dragging all the way up to Programs on the Start menu, and then over and all the way down to Windows Explorer (very inconveniently located at the very bottom of the Programs continuation menu). To create a shortcut for the Explorer, do the following:

1. Click the ⊞Start button on the taskbar.

2. Choose 🔍 Find ▸ on the Start menu.

3. Choose 📄 Files or Folders... on the Find continuation menu.

4. Type **explorer** in the Named edit box of the Find dialog box and press Enter to select the Find Now button.

5. Click the Explorer icon in the Find list box that shows Type as Application to select it.

6. Choose Create Shortcut from the File pull-down menu in the Find dialog box.

7. Drag the Explorer icon in the Find list that shows Type as Shortcut to the desktop and release the mouse button (you may have to scroll down the list to find this shortcut icon) and then close the Find dialog box.

From now on, you can open the Explorer to find files and folders on your hard disk by double-clicking your Shortcut to Explorer icon on the desktop.

For more on the cool uses for shortcuts in Windows, see *Windows 95 For Dummies,* Chapter 4.

Start Menu

The Start menu is the most basic pull-down menu in Windows 95, containing almost all the commands you'll ever need to use.

How do I get to it?

To open the Start menu, you simply click the [Start] button in the lower-left corner of the taskbar or press Ctrl+Esc.

What do I do with it?

The Start menu contains these cool commands (running from bottom to top):

Start Menu Commands	What They Do
Shut Down	Opens the Shut Down Windows dialog box where you can choose among shutting off the computer, restarting the computer, restarting the computer in MS-DOS mode, or, if you're on a LAN (Local Area Network), closing all programs and logging in as a new user.
Run	Opens the Run dialog box where you enter the name of the file, folder, or program that you want to open. If you are unsure about its location on the disk or how to enter its pathname, select the Browse button and then indicate the location of the file, folder, or program on the disk. When you choose OK, Windows fills in its pathname in the Open edit box in the Run Application dialog box (*see* "Installing Programs" and "Starting Programs" in Part III for more on using Run).

(continued)

Start Menu Commands	What They Do
Help	Opens the Help Topics: Windows Help dialog box that contains three tabs: Contents, Index, and Find. Use the Contents tab to look up or print help on general Windows topics. Use the Index tab to search for a specific help topic. Use the Find tab to look up a help topic by searching for a specific word or phrase in the topic (**see** "Getting Help" in Part III).
Find	Opens a continuation menu with the Files or Folders command to locate a particular file or folder on your computer's hard disk, the Computer command to locate a particular computer on your network (**see** "Finding Files and Folders" in Part III), and the On the Microsoft Network command to find stuff on the Microsoft Network (note that this command is not yet implemented in the Preview version of Windows 95).
Settings	Opens a continuation menu with Control Panel to open the Control Panel window (**see** "Control Panel" earlier in Part II), Printers to open the Printers windows (**see** "Printers" in Part V), and Taskbar to open the Taskbar Properties dialog box where you can modify the appearance of the Start menu and the taskbar (**see** "Taskbar" later in Part II).
Documents	Opens a continuation menu containing shortcuts to all your most recently opened files. To open the file (and its associated program, if necessary), you simply choose its shortcut on the continuation menu. To purge this list from time to time and start all over again, choose the Start Menu Programs tab in the Taskbar Properties dialog box and select the Clear button (**see** "Taskbar" later in Part II).
Programs	Opens a continuation menu containing all the programs installed on your computer at the time you installed Windows 95 (including the Windows Accessories — **see** Part IV). To open a particular program, select its menu item (note that many menu items are tied to other continuation menus that you must navigate). You can control which programs appear on the Programs continuation menu by adding folders to or removing folders from the Programs folder.

Deciding what appears on the Start menu

When you install Windows 95 on your computer, it creates a menu item for all the Windows programs installed on your computer (if you're upgrading from Windows 3.1, it converts all your program group windows to menu items on the Programs continuation menu). After that, you can add programs to or remove programs from this menu as you like. The easiest way to do this is as follows:

1. Click [Start] on the taskbar to open the Start menu.

2. Choose [Settings] to open the Settings continuation menu.

3. Choose [Taskbar...] to open the Taskbar Properties dialog box.

4. Choose the Start Menu Programs tab in the Taskbar Properties dialog box.

5. Click the Add button on the Start Menu Programs tab to open the Create Shortcut Wizard and then enter its directory path in the Command line edit box (if you don't have the slightest idea what a directory path is, then click the Browse icon and select the program icon in the Browse window and then choose the Open button or press Enter).

6. Choose the Next> button in the Create Shortcut Wizard or press Enter to open the Select Program Folder dialog box.

7. Make sure that the Programs folder is highlighted in the Select folder to place shortcut in list box (if it's not the highlighted folder, be sure to select it) and then choose Next> or press Enter to open the Select a Title for the Program dialog box.

8. If necessary, edit or replace the program name displayed in the Select a name for the shortcut edit box.

9. After editing the program name (or if the name that Windows 95 chooses is okay), choose the Finish button or press Enter to close the Create Shortcut Wizard and return to the Taskbar Properties dialog box.

10. To add other items, repeat Steps 4 through 9. When you're finished editing items, choose the OK button to close the Taskbar Properties dialog box.

The next time that you open the Programs continuation menu on the Start menu, the item or items you just added by following these steps appear big as day. To remove an item from the Programs continuation menu, you follow the same first four steps for adding an item (*see* the preceding list) and then follow these steps:

5. Choose the Remove button on the Start Menu Programs tab to open the Remove Shortcuts/Folders dialog box.

6. Click the program's icon in the To remove an item from the Start menu, select the item, click Remove list box, and click the Remove button.

7. When you finish removing items from the Programs continuation menu, choose the Close button or press Enter to close the Remove Shortcut/Folders dialog box and then choose OK to close the Taskbar Properties dialog box.

More stuff

You can use the Advanced button located on the Start Menu Programs tab of the Taskbar Properties dialog box to open the Exploring - Start Menu window, where you can quickly remove items from the Programs continuation menu by deleting them from the Programs folder or another folder found within the Programs folder (only the programs in folders contained in the Programs folder show up on the Program continuation menu). To remove an item, select its icon and then press the Del key and choose the Yes button in the Confirm Folder (or File) Delete dialog box.

The Startup folder in the Programs folder contains shortcuts for all the programs that automatically open each time you start Windows 95. To add a new program to this list, click on the Startup folder icon in the All Folders list box which opens the Startup folder. Next, drag a copy of that program's shortcut into Contents of C:\WINDOWS\Start Menu\Programs\Startup list box. To remove a program from this list, drag the program's shortcut icon out of this Contents of list box and onto the desktop (or select its icon and then press Delete to get rid of it).

See also "Taskbar," next.

Taskbar

The taskbar contains the Start button for opening the Start menu as well as buttons for switching among the windows you have open.

How do I get to it?

The taskbar is usually found at the very bottom of the Windows 95 screen (although you can drag it to any of the other three sides of the screen). If you don't happen to see the taskbar on-screen, this means that someone's turned on the Auto hide feature (*see* "Customizing the taskbar" that follows). You must roll the mouse pointer over the area containing the taskbar to make it and its buttons visible on-screen.

Start		4:49 PM

What do I do with it?

The Start button used to open the Start menu (*see* "Start Menu" earlier in Part II) always appears as the first button on the taskbar. In addition, each time you open a program window on the desktop, Windows adds a button representing that program to the taskbar.

These program buttons appear to the right of the Start button in the order in which you opened the programs.

When you minimize a program window, Windows reduces the window to just its button on the taskbar. When a program window is open and active, its button appears pressed on the taskbar. To restore a minimized window and make it the active one, you simply click its button on the taskbar.

You can also bring any open window that's temporarily hidden behind others to the very front and make it active by clicking its button on the taskbar. In other words, you can use the taskbar buttons to quickly switch between the programs you're running in the open windows.

Customizing the taskbar

Normally, the taskbar is always present on the desktop (either on the bottom, top, left, or right side of the screen) and always remains on top of any other window or dialog box that happens to get in its way. You can modify these settings as well as customize the items on the Start menu in the Taskbar Properties dialog box. To open this dialog box, follow these steps:

1. Click ▓Start on the taskbar to open the Start menu.

2. Choose ▓ Settings ▶ to open the Settings continuation menu.

3. Choose ▓ Taskbar... to open the Taskbar Properties dialog box.

You can also open the Taskbar Properties dialog box, shown here, by clicking any area between the taskbar buttons (obviously, if you click any of these buttons, you just end up activating an open window or opening the Start menu) with the secondary mouse button and then choosing the Properties command on the Taskbar context menu.

The Taskbar Properties dialog box contains two tabs: Taskbar Options and Start Menu Programs. The check boxes on the Taskbar Options tab do the following:

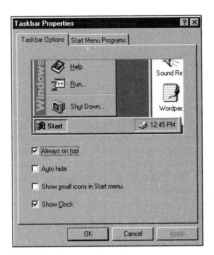

Taskbar Options	What They Do
Always on top	When this box contains a check mark, the taskbar stays in front of any other window or dialog box that it comes in contact with. Deselect this option when you don't want the taskbar to be visible in programs like Word and Excel, even when you run them in full-size windows.
Auto hide	When this box contains a check mark, the taskbar remains invisible on-screen until you roll the mouse pointer somewhere over its position. Select this option when you want to retain access to the taskbar in programs like Word and Excel when you run them in full-size windows without having the taskbar visible.
Show small icons in Start menu	When this box contains a check mark, Windows uses a smaller version of icons on the Start menu options.
Show Clock	When this box contains a check mark, Windows displays the current time at the far-right end of the taskbar.

The command buttons on the Start Menu Programs tab do the following:

Start Menu Programs	What They Do
Add	Opens the Create Shortcut dialog box, where you can specify the pathname of the program that you want to add to the Programs continuation menu. If you don't know the pathname (or anything about pathnames, for that matter), choose the Browse button and select the icon for the program file after locating it in the Browse dialog box.

Start Menu Programs	What They Do
Remove	Opens the Remove Shortcuts/Folders dialog box with a list of all the files on the Programs continuation menu. To remove a file, select its icon and then choose the Delete button.
Advanced	Opens an Exploring - Start Menu window showing the Start Menu and Programs folders. You can then add items to the Programs continuation menu by dragging their icons into the Programs folder. You can remove items by opening the Programs folder and then deleting them.
Clear	Empties the Document continuation menu of all file shortcuts so that Windows can start building a new list of shortcuts.

More stuff

See also "Start Menu," earlier in Part II, and "Switching between Programs," in Part III.

Toolbar

A toolbar (a row of handy buttons for doing routine tasks) appears beneath the window's menu bar when the menu bar is visible.

How do I get to it?

To display a toolbar in a window that has one (like the Exploring or My Computer window), choose Toolbar from the window's View pull-down menu. The following figure shows a toolbar.

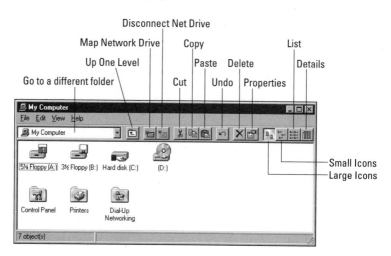

What do I do with it?

Most toolbar buttons are simple regulation buttons that you simply click to make them do whatever it is they do (like switch to small icons). Some toolbars also contain fancy buttons like drop-down list box buttons that let you select a new setting (like the part of the computer to explore an Exploring window) from a list.

More stuff

Toolbars are new in Windows 95, although Microsoft has used them (one might even say overused them) in their Office programs (Word, Excel, PowerPoint, and Access) for a long time. They offer yet another method for doing some of the everyday stuff along with pull-down menus (*see* "Pull-Down Menus" earlier in Part II) and context menus (*see* "Context Menus" earlier in Part II). The biggest draw of a toolbar is that when it's displayed, its buttons are always available for clicking.

Windows

Windows are the boxes that contain all the programs that you run (including any DOS stuff you might still play around with).

How do I get to it?

Each time you open a new program, Windows puts the program in its own *window* that appears on the desktop. Each window contains a title bar with the program icons followed by the name of the window and three sizing buttons: Minimize, Maximize (or Restore if the window's already full-size), and Close. Beneath the title bar, you find the menu bar with all the pull-down menus available in the particular program. If the window is equipped with toolbars and they are visible in the window, you can find them beneath the menu bar.

Below the menu bar and toolbars (if the window's so blessed), you find the contents of the window, which (depending upon the type of window) could consist of a bunch of file and folder icons, word processing documents, spreadsheets, or graphics that you've created. If the size of the window is such that you can't see all of its contents, the window is equipped with either a vertical scroll bar on the right side and/or a horizontal scroll bar at the bottom that you can use to bring new parts of the window into view.

Beneath the optional horizontal scroll bar in some windows, you may also find a status bar bringing up the very bottom. The status bar gives you different sorts of information about the current state of the program. And in some program windows, you'll also meet additional buttons and tools that are truly unique to the application (like the tool and color palettes in the Paint window shown next). If you need to know what these do, you have to resort to using whatever passes for on-line help in that program.

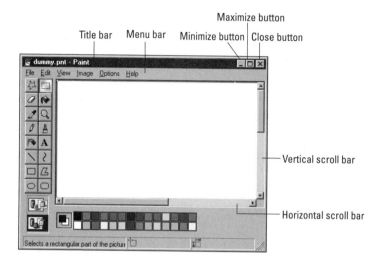

What do I do with it?

Windows can be resized, moved, and rearranged on the desktop to give you more room. Keep in mind that a window must be active before you can select any of its commands or use any of its features. To activate a window, click anywhere on it (the active window is immediately placed on top of the desktop and its title bar becomes highlighted). If not enough of the window is visible for you to click on it, you can always activate the window by clicking its button on the taskbar (*see* "Taskbar" earlier in Part II).

If the window contains a toolbar and you don't have a clue as to what the tool does (many button icons are either too small or just too obscure to decipher), you can get Windows to display the tool's name right below the mouse pointer by positioning the pointer right over the button and waiting patiently.

If the window contains scroll bars, you can use them to display new parts of the window by dragging their scroll boxes (or you can make the window bigger, either manually or with the Maximize button). With a vertical scroll bar, you drag the scroll box up and down:

✦ Drag the scroll box downward to move the items currently displayed upward as you bring new items into view up from the bottom of the window.

✦ Drag the scroll box upward to move the stuff already displayed in the window downward as you bring new items into view down from the top of the window.

With a horizontal scroll bar, you drag the scroll box back and forth to the left and right:

✦ Drag the scroll box to the right to move the stuff already displayed in the window to the left and bring new items into view from the right.

✦ Drag the scroll box to the left to move the stuff already displayed in the window to the right and bring new items into view from the left.

More stuff

See also "Dialog Box," earlier in Part II, for information on dialog boxes (a special form of window).

See also "Control Menu," earlier in Part II, for more on sizing and moving windows.

See also "Taskbar," earlier in Part II, and "Switching between Windows," in Part III, for information on switching between windows.

See also "Arranging the Icons in a Window," in Part III, for more on arranging icons in a window.

See also "Starting Programs," in Part III, for more on opening windows.

See also "Taskbar," earlier in Part II, and "Switching between Programs," in Part III, for more on switching between open windows.

Wizards

A wizard is a set of dialog boxes that leads you through a complex procedure (like installing a new printer or registering your copy of Windows 95 on-line) by asking you a million questions related to your system.

How do I get to it?

Wizards automatically appear when you select a command or double-click an icon whose function is to change some settings or install some new piece of hardware. Some wizard dialog boxes use the term *wizard* in the title bar (like the Add Printer Wizard), while others don't (like Compose New Fax). You can always tell a wizard, however, from a regular dialog box because wizards contain only <Back, Next>, and Cancel buttons.

In the following figure, you see the Add Printer Wizard that walks you through each step necessary to install a new printer on your computer system.

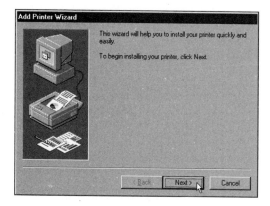

What do I do with it?

Each wizard in Windows 95 is designed to take you through all the steps necessary in changing a group of settings or adding some new hardware. While the questions asked vary according to the particular wizard that's guiding you, you can expect to be forced into making a good number of choices as you proceed through the series of dialog boxes (by clicking the Next> button). If you ever need to refer to some choices made in an earlier dialog box, you can return to the dialog box by clicking the <Back button as many times as necessary to get back to it (once there, you can change your choices if you find it necessary).

Keep in mind that you can abandon the procedure at any time by selecting the Cancel button in a wizard dialog box. However, it's only when you've selected the Finish button in the last wizard dialog box that the group of settings are changed or that the hardware is actually installed on your computer. Canceling anytime prior to the last dialog box guarantees that you'll need to face this wizard again at some later date should you still need to make the setting changes or add the hardware.

More stuff

See also "On-Line Registration," in Part IV, and "Add New Hardware," in Part V, for examples of using a wizard to get something done in Windows 95.

Part III

Doing Everyday Junk in Windows 95

Windows 95 wouldn't be so bad, if you didn't have to know how to do so many different things with it. This part of the book contains an alphabetical listing of all the essential things you'll need to know in order to use Windows 95. Here, you'll find out how to do important stuff like the things mentioned in the following list:

In this part . . .

✔ **Make copies of your really important files.**

✔ **Create new folders to hold the copies of your really important files.**

✔ **Find the folders that hold the copies of your really important files.**

✔ **Open the copies of really important files once you've located their folders.**

✔ **Start all the hundreds of programs that you run under Windows 95.**

✔ **Shut down and get the heck out of Windows 95 after a long day of using all the hundreds of programs you run under Windows 95!**

. . . and much, much more.

Arranging the Icons in a Window

Get wayward icons back in line or sort them in a particular order (by name, date, and that sort of thing) in a window.

How do I do it?

To line up icons when they're arranged willy-nilly in a window, choose Line Up Icons from the View pull-down menu or from the window's context menu.

To arrange icons in a particular order:

1. Choose Arrange Icons from the View pull-down menu or from the window's context menu.

2. Choose the way you want the icons ordered from the Arrange Icons continuation menu: by Name, by Type, by Size, by Date, or Auto Arrange (to let Windows figure it out).

When do I do it?

Normally, Windows arranges the icons in a window by their type (which is determined by the filename extension and is normally hidden from view). Use the Arrange Icons command whenever you want to overrule this regular arrangement (and choose the Auto Arrange command when you want to return to it).

More stuff

See also "Icons," in Part II, for more on icons.

Changing the View Options for a Window

Modify the size of the icons used in a window to represent files and folders and determine how much (if any) information about them is displayed.

How do I do it?

You can change which icons are used and how much information is displayed about the files and folders they represent by selecting the following options from either the window's View pull-down menu or its context menu:

→ **Large Icons (the default):** displays the largest version of the folder and file icons with their names below.

→ **Small Icons:** displays a smaller version of the folder and file icons with their names on the right side of the icons.

✦ **List:** uses the same icons as the Small Icons option except that the icons with their folder and filenames are arranged in a single column along the left side of the window.

✦ **Details:** adds columns of additional information (like a description or the file type, file size, and the like) to the arrangement used when you select the List option.

When do I do it?

Switch to the Small Icons viewing option when you need to see as much of the contents of a window as possible. Switch to the Details viewing option when you need to get as much information as possible about the files and folder in a window.

More stuff

See also "Icons," in Part II, for more on icons.

See also "Arranging the Icons in a Window," earlier in this part.

Copying Files and Folders

In Windows 95, you can copy files and folders to new folders or disks with either drag and drop or copy and paste.

How do I do it?

To copy files with drag and drop, you follow these steps:

1. Open the window that contains the items to be copied and the one with the folder or disk to which the items are to be copied.

2. Select all the items to be copied.

3. Hold down the Ctrl key as you drag the selected items to the folder to which you want them copied.

4. When the destination folder icon is selected (that is, highlighted), drop the selected items by releasing the mouse button.

To copy files with copy and paste, you follow these steps:

1. Open the window that holds the items to be copied.

2. Select all the items to be copied and then choose the Copy command from the Edit pull-down menu or press Ctrl+C.

3. Open the window that holds the folder or disk where the copied items are to appear.

4. Open the folder or disk to hold the copied items and then choose the Paste command from the Edit pull-down menu or press Ctrl+V.

When do I do it?

Use drag and drop to copy when you have both the folder with the items to be copied and the destination folder or disk displayed on the desktop (as when using the Explorer). Use copy and paste to copy when you can't easily display both the folder with the items to be copied and the destination folder or disk together on the desktop.

More stuff

See also "Explorer," in Part II, for more on copying.

See also "Selecting Files and Folders," later in this part, for information about selecting files and folders in a window.

Creating New Files and Folders

Create empty folders to hold your files and empty files to hold new documents of a particular type right within Windows 95.

How do I do it?

To create an empty folder, follow these steps:

1. Open the window and the folder in which the new folder is to appear.

2. Choose New from the File pull-down menu or the window's context menu.

3. Choose Folder from the New continuation menu.

4. Replace the temporary folder name (New Folder) by typing a name of your choosing and pressing Enter.

To create an empty file of a certain type, follow these steps:

1. Open the window and the folder where the new file is required.

2. Choose New from the File pull-down menu or the window's context menu.

3. Choose the type of file you want to create (MS PowerPoint 4.0 Presentation, Microsoft Excel 5.0 Worksheet, Microsoft Word 6.0 Document, Wave Sound, Text Document, Rich Text File, Bitmap Image, or WordPerfect 6.0 Document) from the New continuation menu.

4. Replace the temporary filename (like New Microsoft Word 6.0 Document) by typing a name of your choosing and pressing Enter.

5. To open the application associated with the new file, double-click the file icon (Microsoft Excel 5.0 Worksheet opens Excel 5.0, Microsoft Word 6.0 Document opens Word 6.0, Wave Sound opens the Sound Recorder accessory, Text Document opens the Notepad accessory, Rich Text File opens the WordPad accessory, Bitmap opens the Paint accessory, and WordPerfect Document (6.0) opens WordPerfect 6.0 for Windows).

When do I do it?

Create a new folder when you need to have a new place to store your files and other folders. Create an empty file when you're at the desktop level and want to name a file in a particular folder before you create it.

More stuff

See also "Long Filenames," in Part II, for information on naming new files and folders in Window 95.

Deleting Junk

Get rid of any unneeded files and folders to free up storage space on your computer.

How do I do it?

To delete files or folders, follow these steps:

1. Open the folder that holds the files or folders to be deleted.

2. Select all the files and folders to be deleted.

3. Choose Delete from the File pull-down menu or press the Del key (you can also drag the selected items to the Recycle Bin).

Windows 95 puts all items that you delete in the Recycle Bin. To get rid of all the items in the Recycle Bin, do the following:

1. Double-click the Recycle Bin icon and then choose Empty Recycle Bin from the File pull-down menu (or simply choose Empty Recycle Bin from the Recycle Bin icon's context menu).

2. Choose the Yes button or press Enter in the Confirm File Delete or Confirm Multiple File Delete dialog box (just be aware that there's no turning back from this step).

When do I do it?

Get rid of stuff in the Recycle Bin only when you're absolutely sure that you're never going to need it again (or you have backed up the files on floppy disks or some other media such as tapes or CD-ROMs).

More stuff

See also "Recycle Bin," in Part II.

See also "Uninstalling Programs," later in this part, for information on getting rid of a program.

See also "System Tools," in Part IV, for information on backing up files before you get rid of them.

Doing DOS Stuff

Just in case you haven't had enough of DOS in the past, you can open a window with a DOS prompt in Windows 95 and type DOS commands to your heart's content.

How do I do it?

To open a window to DOS within Windows 95, you follow these steps:

1. Click `Start` on the taskbar.

2. Drag up to `Programs` ▶ on the Start menu.

3. Drag over and down to `MS-DOS Prompt` on the Programs continuation menu.

To restart your computer in DOS mode (heaven forbid) rather than in Windows 95, you follow these steps:

1. Click `Start` on the taskbar.

2. Choose `Shut Down...` on the Start menu.

3. Choose the Restart the computer in MS-DOS mode? radio button in the Shut Down Windows dialog box.

4. Choose the Yes button in the Shut Down Windows dialog box.

To return to Windows 95 after restarting in MS-DOS mode, type **exit** at the DOS prompt and then press Enter.

You can also restart Windows 95 from the DOS prompt by typing **win** and pressing the Enter key. If you type **win** rather than **exit,** you encounter the following message:

```
You are currently running in MS-DOS mode. Do you
want to return to normal mode, to run Windows
applications again [Enter=Y, Esc=N]
```

Press the Enter key to get the heck out of DOS and restart your computer in the safety and comfort of Windows 95, or press Esc if you're a masochist and want to keep entering DOS commands!

When do I do it?

Don't fool around with DOS commands unless you have no choice and are really sure of what you're doing. If you ever get a DOS window open and then get cold feet, just click the Close button in the MS-DOS Prompt window to close it and get back to Windows 95 where you belong.

You can also close the MS-DOS Prompt window within Windows 95 or restart the computer from MS-DOS mode by typing **exit** at the DOS prompt and pressing the Enter key.

More stuff

For more on using DOS in Windows 95, see *Windows 95 For Dummies,* Chapter 14.

Finding Files and Folders

The Find feature enables you to quickly locate all those misplaced files and folders that you're just sure are hiding somewhere on your hard disk.

How do I do it?

To open the Find window to search for a file or folder, follow these steps:

1. Click [Start] on the taskbar.

2. Choose [Find] on the Start menu.

3. Choose [Files or Folders...] on the Find continuation menu to open the Find: All Files window.

4. Enter the search conditions and where to look in the appropriate tabs of the Find: All Files window (Name & Location, Date Modified, and Advanced, *see* "Telling Windows what to look for," which follows this section).

5. Select the Find Now button or press Enter to start the search.

When Windows 95 completes a search, it expands the Find dialog box to display all the files that meet your search conditions in a list box. This list box shows the name, location, size, type, and the date the file was last modified. If this information isn't enough for you to make a positive ID on the file, use the Quick View command on the file icon's context menu to take a gander at the file's contents (*see* "Getting a Quick View of a File's Contents" in this part).

Telling Windows what to look for

The Find dialog box contains three tabs (Name & Location, Date Modified, and Advanced) with various options in which you set the search conditions to be used. On the tabs in the Find dialog box, you find these options:

```
Find: Files named start                                    _ □ ✕
File   Edit   View   Options   Help

 ┌ Name & Location ┐ Date Modified │ Advanced │
                                                      ┌─────────────┐
                                                      │   Find Now  │
   Named:  start                              ▼       └─────────────┘
                                                      ┌─────────────┐
                                                      │    Stop     │
   Look in:  Hard disk (C:)         ▼    Browse...    └─────────────┘
                                                      ┌─────────────┐
              ☑ Include subfolders                    │ New Search  │
                                                      └─────────────┘
                                                            🔍
```

Name	In Folder	Size	Type
Startup	C:\WINDOWS	2KB	Microsoft Program Gr...
Start Menu	C:\WINDOWS		Folder
jmpstart	C:\WINDOWS	1KB	Configuration Settings
Start	C:\WINDOWS\CO...	8KB	Application

```
18 file(s) found
```

Name & Location Tab Options	What They Do
Named	Enter all or part of the file or folder name you're looking for in this edit box. Don't worry about how the name is capitalized.
	Windows remembers the stuff you enter in this edit box so that it can reselect search text in the drop-down list box. To search for all files of a certain type (like all the Excel worksheets on a disk) enter an asterisk (*) followed by a period and the three-character extension (which, although it can be searched, is not displayed in Windows 95) used by the program to identify its own (as in ***.xls** to search for all Excel worksheet files).
Look in	Use this drop-down list box to select the drive where you want the search conducted.
Include subfolders	Normally, Windows searches all the folders within the folders on the disk specified in the Look in edit box. If you're pretty sure that the files and folders you want won't be found any deeper than in the first level of folders, remove the check mark from this check box.

Date Modified Tab Options	*What They Do*
All Files	Normally, Windows automatically selects this radio button and searches all files on the location specified in the Look in edit box on the Name & Location tab. If you selected the Find all files created or modified radio button (see the following) for the last search and now want to search all files, don't forget to reselect this radio button.
Find all files created or modified	Select this radio button to find files or folders created or modified between certain dates or within the last few days or months (see the following options).
between and	Select this radio button and enter the two dates between which the files or folders must have been created or edited. The two dates you enter in the between edit boxes are included in the search.
during the previous month(s)	Select this radio button and enter the number of months in the edit box to search for files and folders created or modified within a set number of months.
during the previous day(s)	Select this radio button and enter the number of days in the edit box to search for files and folders created or modified within a set number of days.

Advanced Tab Options	*What They Do*
Of type	Use this drop-down list box to specify a particular type of file to search for (rather than all files and folders, which is the default).
Containing text	Use this edit box to specify a string of characters, a word, or a phrase that should be contained within the files you're looking for.
Size in K	Select the At least or At most option in the drop-down list box and enter the number of K (kilobytes) that the size of the files to be searched must have attained or not exceeded.

Keep in mind that the search conditions you cook up with the Name & Location, Date Modified, and Advanced tabs of the Find dialog box are cumulative. This means that if you want to find all files and folders created within the last six days but you have the name *klondike* still entered in the Named edit box of the Name & Location tab, Windows searches only for files and folders that use the name *klondike* in their file and folder names and have been created or modified within the last six days. To find all the files, regardless of what they're called, you need to delete *klondike* from the Named edit box and then choose the Find Now button again.

If you want to return all the search settings to their default values before you conduct another search, choose the New Search button in the Find dialog box and then choose OK in the Find Files alert box.

When do I do it?

The Find feature in Windows 95 is so quick (even when searching an entire hard disk that's just chock-full of junk) that I urge you to use it whenever you're having the least little bit of trouble locating a file or folder (rather than waste a bunch of time wading through even the more likely files and folders). Keep in mind that you don't have to know the name of the file to use the Find feature, as Windows 95 can search for specific text in a file if you use the Containing text edit box on the Advanced tab of the Find dialog box.

More stuff

For more on finding files, see *Windows 95 For Dummies,* Chapter 8.

Formatting a Disk

Floppy disks fresh from the box must be formatted before you can save files and folders on them.

How do I do it?

To format a floppy disk in drive A or B of your computer, follow these steps:

1. Insert a blank floppy disk or a disk that holds files and folders that you don't give a hoot about.

2. Double-click the My Computer button to open the My Computer window.

3. Click the icon for the Floppy drive (A: or B:) in the My Computer window with the secondary mouse button (the button you don't normally use) to open its context menu.

4. Select the For<u>m</u>at command from the drive's context menu to open the Format dialog box.

5. By default, Windows 95 selects high density [1.2MB (5.25") for 5¹/₄-inch disks or 1.44MB (3.5") for 3¹/₂-inch disks] as the Capacity for the size of the floppy disk you're formatting. Choose the lesser (double-density) capacity [360K (5.25") for 5¹/₄-inch disks or 720K (3.5") for 3¹/₂-inch disks] if you inserted that kind of disk in your floppy drive.

6. By default, Windows 95 chooses <u>Q</u>uick (erase) as the Format Type. If you're formatting a brand new floppy, choose the <u>F</u>ull radio button. If you're creating a backup disk and have been directed to make a boot disk, choose the Copy system files only radio button.

7. If you want to label the floppy disk, enter a label in the Label edit box. If you decide not to use the label entered in the Label edit box, you can select the No Label check box.

8. If you want to see a Format Results dialog box giving you the lowdown on the disk's storage status after the formatting is completed (such as total capacity, bytes in bad sectors, and bytes used by the system), select the Display summary when finished check box.

9. Choose the Start button to begin formatting the disk.

Format - 3½ Floppy (A:)	? X
Capacity:	
1.44 Mb (3.5") ▼	Start
Format type	Close
● Quick (erase)	
○ Full	
○ Copy system files only	
Other options	
Label:	
☐ No label	
☑ Display summary when finished	
☐ Copy system files	

After you click Start, Windows keeps you informed of its progress in the Formatting box at the bottom of the Format dialog box. If you need to stop the process before it's complete, choose the Cancel button.

When the disk formatting is finished, select the Close button or press Enter to close the Format dialog box or, if you want to format another disk of the same type, replace the newly formatted disk with another that needs formatting and choose the Start button (or press Enter) to begin formatting it.

Be sure to match the capacity setting to the physical type of disk you're using: double-sided double-density [360K (5.25") for 5¼-inch disks and 720K (3.5") for 3½-inch disks] versus double-sided quad-density [or high-density; 1.2MB (5.25") for 5¼-inch disks and 1.44 MB (3.5") for 3½-inch disks].

When do I do it?

Use the Quick (erase) format type when reformatting a disk that contains files and folders that you no longer need to have around. Use the Full format type when formatting a blank disk for the first time (that is, one that's right out of the box).

More stuff

TIP

You can also format a brand new, never-been-formatted, right-out-of-the-box diskette by inserting it in its disk drive and then double-clicking the drive icon in the My Computer window. Windows 95 will then display the alert box containing this message:

The disk in drive A (or B, depending upon which one you double-clicked) is not formatted. Do you want to format it now?

Choose the Yes button or press Enter to open the Format dialog box, where you can specify the disk capacity, format type, label, and so on before you start the formatting with the Start button.

Getting a Quick View of a File's Contents

Quick View lets you have a fast look-see into the contents of certain types of files before you open them.

How do I do it?

Click the file's icon with the secondary mouse button and select the Quick View command from its context menu. Note that if the file's context menu doesn't have a Quick View command, that file is of a type that Windows 95 can't peek inside, and you just have to take a chance and open up the file to see whether it's the one you want to use.

When do I do it?

Use Quick View whenever you just can't figure out from the filename alone whether or not the file you've located is the one you really want to open.

	A	B	C
1	Three Little Pigs Building Supply -- Client List		
2	Last Name	First Name	Street
3	Andersen	Christian	340 The Shadow
4	Andersen	Hans	341 The Shadow
5	Appleseed	Johnny	6789 Fruitree Tr
6	Baggins	Bingo	99 Hobbithole
7	Baum	L. Frank	447 Toto Too Rd
8	Brown	Charles	59 Flat Plains
9	Bryant	Michael	326 Chef's Lane
10	Cassidy	Butch	Sundance Kidde
11	Cinderella	Poore	8 Lucky Maiden Way
12	Cupid	Eros	97 Mount Olympus
13	Dragon	Kai	2 Pleistocene Era
14	Eaters	Big	444 Big Pigs Court

Clients.wk1 - Quick View

File   View   Help

More stuff

To open a file from the Quick View window so that you can edit it, click the Open File for Editing button on the window's toolbar or choose Open file for Editing on the File pull-down menu. To be able to use Quick View to snoop in a bunch of different files without opening separate windows for each file, click the Replace Window button on the window's toolbar or choose Replace Window on the View pull-down menu.

See also "Context Menus," in Part II, for more on using context menus.

See also "Finding Files and Folders," earlier in this part, for information about using the Find feature to locate files.

Getting Help

On-line help is always just a couple of clicks away, although how much help is available on any one topic depends on just what topic you're looking up.

How do I do it?

To open the Help Topics dialog box, follow these steps:

1. Click [🔠 Start] on the taskbar.

2. Choose [🔵 Help] on the Start menu to open the Help Topics: Windows Help dialog box.

3. Select a help topic in the Contents tab list box, the Index tab list box, or the Find tab list box and then choose the Display button or press the Enter key.

4. Read the help in the Windows Help window that appears. To print the Help topic, choose the Options button and then choose Print Topic from the pull-down menu. To close the Windows Help window, click the window's Close button.

When do I do it?

You can narrow much of the on-line help in Windows 95 to the task at hand by selecting the Help or ? button that appears in the dialog box or window you have open. Leave the searching for topics in the Help Topics: Windows Help dialog box to times when you need general assistance in using a Windows 95 feature.

More stuff

Many Help topic windows in Windows 95 help have a little shortcut button in the text (a button with a curved arrow pointing up and to the left). When you click this button, Windows opens the dialog box or window that's being described in the text so that you can go ahead and make any necessary changes.

Getting the Lowdown on a Disk

Checking the properties for a disk can give you quick information about the size of the disk and how much space is used and how much is free, as well as let you use a few disk tools or set up disk-sharing on a network.

How do I do it?

Open the My Computer or Explorer window, click the icon for the disk you want to know about with the secondary mouse button, and then choose Properties from the disk's context menu to open the *such 'n' such* disk Properties dialog box.

Hard disk (C:) Properties   ? ☒

| General | Tools | Sharing |

Label: HARD DISK

Type: Local Disk

■ Used space: 296,476,672 bytes 282MB

☐ Free space: 40,312,832 bytes 38.4MB

Capacity: 336,789,504 bytes 321MB

Drive C

[OK]   [Cancel]   [Apply]

The General tab in this Properties dialog box shows you the name of the disk (or its label, in the case of floppy disks), the amount of used and free space on the disk, and the disk's total storage capacity (topped off with a great big pie chart).

The Properties dialog boxes for disks also contain Tools and Sharing tabs:

✦ The Tools tab contains a Check Now button for checking the disk for errors, a Backup Now button for backing up the contents of the disk with the Microsoft Backup utility, and a Defragment Now button to rearrange the files on the disk in contiguous blocks.

✦ The Sharing tab contains a bunch of buttons and boxes for letting people on your LAN (Local Area Network) have access to the precious data on your hard disk. When setting up file-sharing, you can determine whether they get full access or read-only access and whether they must know the secret password in order to get this access (of course, you'll want your network administrator to determine all this stuff for you).

When do I do it?

Consult a disk's properties whenever you need to find out stuff like how much storage space is still free (in a cool pie chart form) or when you need to check the disk for errors, back it up, or defragment its data.

More stuff

For information about opening up the My Computer and Exploring windows, *see* "My Computer" and "Explorer" in Part II.

See also "Context Menus" and "Properties" in Part II.

For more on backing up data from disks with the Microsoft Backup utility and defragmenting disks with the Disk Defragmenter, *see* "System Tools" in Part IV.

Getting the Lowdown on a File

Checking the properties for a file can give you quick information about what application created the file, the size and location of the file, and the date the file was created, last modified, and most recently opened.

How do I do it?

Open the folder in the My Computer or Exploring window that contains the file you want information about, click the file icon with the secondary mouse button, and then choose Properties from the file's context menu to open the *such 'n' such* file Properties dialog box.

```
Sales Summary 1994 Properties                    ? X
 General | Summary | Statistics |

     [icon]      Sales Summary 1994

  Type:       Microsoft Excel 5.0 Worksheet
  Location:   EXCELCBT
  Size:       77.5KB (79,360 bytes)

  MS-DOS name:   SALESS~1.XLS
  Created:       (unknown)
  Modified:      Tuesday, December 14, 1993
  Accessed:      Wednesday, August 17, 1994

  Attributes:      [ ] Read-only     [ ] Hidden
                   [x] Archive       [ ] System

              [   OK   ]  [  Cancel  ]  [ Apply ]
```

Depending upon the type of file (document versus program and the type of document it is), the file's Properties dialog box contains different tabs. All Properties dialog boxes for files, however, have a General tab that tells you such things as

+ The file's Windows 95 filename

+ The file's type

+ The file's folder location

+ File size in bytes

+ The file's DOS filename (using the infamous eight-dot-three filename system)

+ The file's creation date

+ The date the file was last edited (modified)

+ The date the file was last opened on your computer (accessed)

+ The file's attributes: Read-only, Archive, Hidden, and System (please don't fool with the attributes unless you're certain that you know what you're doing)

When do I do it?

Check a file's properties whenever you're uncertain as to what type of file it is (program versus document) or need specific information about its size and/or the date the file was created, last modified, or last opened.

More stuff

See also "My Computer" and "Explorer," in Part II, for information about opening up the My Computer and Exploring windows.

See also "Context Menus" and "Properties," in Part II.

Installing Programs

Windows 95 includes an installation Wizard as well as a Run command on the Start menu that you can use to install new software programs on your computer.

How do I do it?

To install a new program from floppy disks or a CD-ROM by using the Install Wizard, you follow these steps:

1. Click 🏁 Start on the taskbar.

2. Choose 🔧 Settings ▶ on the Start menu.

3. Choose 🖥 Control Panel ▶ on the Settings continuation menu to open the Control Panel window.

Add/Remove
Programs

4. Double-click Add/Remove Programs in the Control Panel to open the Add/Remove Programs Properties dialog box.

5. Select the Install button in the Add/Remove Programs Properties dialog box and then follow the steps as outlined in the Install Program From Floppy or CD-ROM Wizard.

Isn't there another way?

You can also use the Run command on the Start menu to install a program from the Run dialog box. In the Open edit box, you need to enter the drive letter that contains the disk or CD-ROM from which the program will be installed, followed by a colon and the name of the installation program (either **setup** or **install**). For example, to install a new CD-ROM game that uses *install* as its installation command, you enter

d:\install

in the Open edit box of the Run Application dialog box and then choose the OK button or press Enter.

When do I do it?

Use the Install Wizard to install all new Windows 95 versions of software (also known as 32-bit versions of a program). Install programs from the Run dialog box when you are installing older software whose installation instructions talk about entering an **install** or **setup** command in the Run dialog box (it's only recently turned into Run Application in Windows 95).

More stuff

See also "Add/Remove Programs," in Part V.

Moving Files and Folders

In Windows 95, you move files and folders around either by dragging and dropping them or by cutting and pasting them.

How do I do it?

To move files and folders with drag and drop, use these steps:

1. Open a window that contains the folders and files that you want to move. If you're just moving some files in a folder, be sure to open that folder in the window.

2. Open a window that displays the icon for the folder or disk to which the files and folders you're about to select in the first folder (described in Step 1) will be moved.

3. Select all the files and folders in the first window that are to be moved.

4. Drag the selected files and folders from the first window to the window that contains the destination folder or disk (the one where the files are to be moved).

5. As soon as you select the icon of the destination folder or disk (indicated by a highlighted name), release the mouse button to move the files into that folder or disk.

When you drag files or folders from one disk to another, Windows 95 automatically copies the files and folders rather than moving them (meaning that you must still delete them from their original disk if you need the space). If you want to copy files between folders on the same disk with drag and drop, you must hold down the Ctrl key as you drag the file and folder icons.

Isn't there another way?

To move files and folders with cut and paste, use these steps:

1. Open a window that displays all the files and folders to be moved.

2. Select all the files and folders to be moved.

3. Choose the Cut command from the Edit pull-down menu of the window or press Ctrl+X to cut the selected file(s) and place them in the Clipboard.

4. Open a window that contains the destination folder or disk (the one to which you want to move the selected files or folders).

5. Choose the Paste command from the Edit pull-down menu of the window where the selected stuff is to be moved or press Ctrl+V to insert the file(s) into the folder open in the Contents of pane.

When using the Cut and Paste commands to move files or folders, you don't have to keep the first window in which they were originally located open after you cut them. Just be sure that you paste cut files or folders in a location before you use the Copy or Cut command again in Windows 95.

When do I do it?

Use the drag-and-drop method when you can see both the files and folders to be moved and the folder to which you are moving them on the desktop. Switch to the cut-and-paste method when this is not the case.

More stuff

See also "Explorer," in Part II, for specific steps on moving files with the drag-and-drop and cut-and-paste methods in the Exploring window.

See also "Selecting Files and Folders," in this part, for information about selecting files and folders for moving.

Moving and Resizing Windows

You can move windows around the desktop and resize them (from full-screen all the way down to little tiny buttons on the taskbar) at your convenience.

How do I do it?

To move a window, follow these steps:

1. If necessary, restore the window to an in-between size either by clicking ▣ if the window is maximized or by clicking its button on the taskbar if the window is minimized.

2. Position the mouse pointer over the window's title bar.

3. Drag the outline of the window to its new location on the desktop.

4. Release the mouse button to drop the window in its new location on the desktop.

When resizing a window, you can select anything from a full-size version that takes up the entire screen and blots out everything else on the desktop (when it's referred to as *maximized*) all the way down to a mere button on the taskbar (when it's called *minimized*).

To maximize a window, you have two methods to choose from:

✦ Click ▢ on the window's title bar.

✦ Choose Maximize from the window's Control Menu.

Remember that after you maximize a window, you can restore the window to its original size by doing one of these two things:

✦ Click ▣ on the window's title bar.

✦ Choose Restore from the window's Control Menu.

To minimize a window to just a button on the taskbar, you can do either of the following:

✦ Click ▯ on the window's title bar.

✦ Choose Minimize from the window's Control Menu.

In addition to using the automatic sizing controls, you can manually size a window (assuming that it's not currently minimized or maximized) by dragging any of its sides or corners. You can always tell when Windows 95 will allow you to move one or more of the sides of a window by dragging because the mouse pointer changes from the standard pointer to a double-headed arrow.

When do I do it?

Move a window whenever something else (like the taskbar or another window) gets in the way so that you can't see its contents. Maximize a window when you're doing some serious work (or playing) in that window and don't need the distraction of all the other junk that populates the Windows 95 desktop. Minimize a window when you still need it open (especially when it's running processes like printing or calculating in the background) but won't be directly using its features for a while. Keep the window sized in between when you need to see part of its contents on the desktop at the same time (as when moving or copying with drag and drop).

More stuff

See also "Control Panel," in Part II, for information on how to use the Control Menu to size and move windows.

See also "Taskbar," in Part II, and "Switching between Programs," later in this part, for more on using the buttons on the taskbar.

See also "Windows," in Part II, for more stuff about the different parts of windows.

Opening Files and Folders

You open folders to get the files they contain, and you open files to get at the stuff they contain.

How do I do it?

The most common way to open a file or folder is to double-click its icon on the desktop or in the window where it's located.

Isn't there another way?

You can also open a file or folder by clicking its file or folder icon with the secondary mouse button and then choosing the Open command at the top of its context menu.

Remember: If you're using the Explorer, you open folders shown in the All Folders pane on the left side of the Explorer by single-clicking the folder's icon. However, to open a folder shown in the Contents of pane on the right side of the Explorer, you must double-click the folder's icon to open it (single-clicking only succeeds in selecting the folder without opening it).

When do I do it?

Open a file on the desktop when you want to use the file and start the application that created the file (assuming that it's not already running). Open a folder when you want to delete some of its contents or move or copy the folder to another folder or disk.

More stuff

See also "Context Menus," in Part II, for more information about using context menus.

See also "Selecting Files and Folders," in this part, for information about selecting files and folders after the folder is open.

Playing CDs

With a CD-ROM drive, a sound card, and some cool speakers, you can listen to music while you work or play great multimedia CD-ROMs like Iron Helix on your lunch hour and breaks.

How do I do it?

Today's CD-ROM drives can play audio CDs (compact discs) as well as CD-ROMs with multimedia programs like encyclopedias and games, games, games.

To play the latest Madonna or Nirvana compact disc in your CD-ROM player, follow these steps:

1. Insert the CD (the shiny side with rainbows and no writing facing down) in the CD-ROM drive.

2. When you close the door on the CD-ROM drive, Windows reads information that tells it that the CD is of the audio (compact disc) type rather than the data (CD-ROM) type and then automatically opens the CD Player window (like the one shown in the next figure).

3. To start playing the compact disc, click the play button (the one with the triangle pointing to the right). To pause the CD, click the pause button (the one with two vertical bars). To eject the CD, click the eject button (the one with the triangle pointing up over a single horizontal bar).

Note that you can control the volume for the CD Player (as well as the volume for any of the stuff connected to your sound card) in the Volume Control window. To open this window from the CD Player window, choose <u>V</u>olume Control at the very bottom of the <u>V</u>iew pull-down menu.

If you place a CD-ROM that has some multimedia program or game in your CD-ROM drive, Windows 95 automatically opens a window showing the folders and files on the drive (usually D:\ on most computers) instead of opening the CD Player.

If this is the first time you've used the multimedia program, you probably need to install it. If you see a window icon named Install in the D:\ window, double-click it to install the program. After you install the program, double-click the program's icon in the D:\ window to start the program or game.

When do I do it?

You can play audio CDs in the background while doing other stuff (like writing a letter in your word processor or updating an expense account in your spreadsheet program). Depending upon the type of CD-ROM program you have, you may be able to pause the program while you do other stuff in Windows 95 (however, some games won't let you pause or save your place, and you may get yourself good and killed if you activate another program window or go to the desktop to do something).

More stuff

See also "Multimedia," in Part IV, and "Multimedia" and "Sounds," in Part V, for information about changing the sound and multimedia settings for your computer.

Renaming Files and Folders

You can rename file and folder icons directly in Windows 95 by typing over the file or folder name.

How do I do it?

To rename a file or folder, follow these steps:

1. Open the window that contains the folder or file you want to rename.

2. Locate the icon for the file or folder.

3. Click the name of the file or folder to be renamed to select just its filename text or choose Rena<u>m</u>e on the <u>F</u>ile pull-down menu to select its filename.

4. Type the new name that you want to give the folder (up to 255 characters).

If you have trouble just selecting the file or folder name (you often end up selecting the entire icon, name and all), use the Rena<u>m</u>e command on the window's <u>F</u>ile pull-down menu or the icon's context menu to select the name. Also, after the file or folder name is selected, doing any typing entirely replaces the current name. If you want to edit the file or folder name rather than replace it, you need to click the insertion point at the place in the name that needs editing before you begin typing.

When do I do it?

Rename files and folders whenever you feel that they need more appropriate or descriptive names. Just be careful not to rename files and folders that are referred to in shortcuts, as doing so messes them up permanently (*see* "Shortcuts" in Part II).

More stuff

For more on renaming files and folders, see *Windows 95 For Dummies,* Chapter 12.

Selecting Files and Folders

To select files and folders in Windows 95 for doing such things as copying, moving, or removing, you must select their icons.

How do I do it?

You select files and folders on the desktop and in open windows by using the following mouse techniques:

✦ To select a single file or folder, click its icon.

✦ To select a bunch of separate files or folders, hold down the Ctrl key as you click each file's or folder's icon.

✦ To select a bunch of files or folders whose icons are located all in a row or next to each other in some way, click the first file or folder icon and then hold down the Shift key as you click the last file or folder icon in the bunch.

You can also select a bunch of files or folders that are all next to one another by dragging a bounding box around the whole group. To do so

1. Position the mouse pointer slightly above and to the left of the first file or folder icon.

2. Drag the mouse diagonally down and to the right. As you drag, Windows 95 draws a bounding box and selects all the file or folder icons within this box.

3. As soon as the last file or folder in the bunch you want selected is highlighted, you can release the mouse button.

To select all the files in a folder, choose Select <u>A</u>ll from the <u>E</u>dit pull-down menu or press Ctrl+A.

When do I do it?

You must select files and folders before you can do any of the following stuff to them:

✦ Open them up

✦ Move or copy them to a new folder or disk

✦ Get rid of them

✦ Get information about them (that is, properties)

✦ Rename them

More stuff

See also "Icons" in Part II.

See also "Copying Files and Folders," "Getting the Lowdown on a File," "Moving Files and Folders," "Opening Files and Folders," and "Renaming Files and Folders," all in this part, for more information on the things you normally do after selecting files and folders.

Shutting Down Windows 95

Windows 95 includes a shut-down procedure that you should follow before you pull the plug on your machine.

How do I do it?

To shut down Windows 95 so that you can shut off your computer and get home to the kids, follow these steps:

1. Click 🟦Start on the taskbar.

2. Choose 🔲 Shut Down... on the Start menu to open the Shut Down Windows dialog box.

3. To completely shut down Windows and power down your computer, choose the Yes button or press Enter.

✦ To restart the computer (which you often have to do after installing a new piece of hardware or software), choose the Restart the computer? radio button before you choose the Yes button.

✦ To restart the computer in DOS mode, choose the Restart the computer in MS-DOS mode? radio button before you choose the Yes button.

✦ To log onto the networked computer as a different user (and change the computer settings to match your user profile), choose the Close all programs and log on as a different user? radio button before you choose the Yes button.

```
┌─────────────────────────────────────────────────────────┐
│ Shut Down Windows                                    [×]  │
├─────────────────────────────────────────────────────────┤
│  🖳   Are you sure you want to:                           │
│                                                           │
│        ⦿ Shut down the computer?                          │
│        ○ Restart the computer?                            │
│        ○ Restart the computer in MS-DOS mode?             │
│        ○ Close all programs and log on as a different user?│
│                                                           │
│            ┌─────────┐  ┌─────────┐  ┌─────────┐          │
│            │   Yes   │  │   No    │  │  Help   │          │
│            └─────────┘  └─────────┘  └─────────┘          │
└─────────────────────────────────────────────────────────┘
```

When do I do it?

✦ Choose the Shut down the computer? option in the Shut Down Windows dialog box right before you're ready to turn off the machine so that you go can home and have a real life.

✦ Choose the Restart the computer? option when you've installed some new software or hardware and the installation program tells you that you must restart the machine before you can use the newly installed stuff.

You can also use this option in the unlikely event that Windows 95 becomes so screwed up that you need to restart the whole shebang (for instance, all the colors on the desktop get messed up and go all magenta and green on you).

✦ Don't ever choose the Restart the computer in <u>M</u>S-DOS mode? option unless you are inexplicably possessed by a need to type some DOS commands or take one last look at that ugly old DOS prompt.

✦ Choose the <u>C</u>lose all programs and log on as a different user? option when you're on a network, you share your computer with others, and one of these others has already beaten you to the machine.

When you use this option, Windows presents you with the Enter Network Password dialog box, where you need to enter your user name in the <u>U</u>ser name edit box and, if you have one, your password in the <u>P</u>assword edit box. After you supply this information and choose OK, Windows logs you onto the computer using your user profile, which customizes Windows to your specifications (including such things as which shortcuts are displayed on the desktop, which programs are displayed on the Start menu, and which color scheme and wallpaper pattern are used).

More stuff

When you select the <u>S</u>hut down the computer? option in the Shut Down Windows dialog box, Windows 95 displays a screen telling you that you can safely turn off the power to your computer. Should you decide that you want to restart the computer at that point, hold down Ctrl+Alt+Del (the old three-finger salute in DOS!) to restart Windows 95.

When you select the <u>S</u>hut down the computer? option in the Shut Down Windows dialog box on a computer connected to a LAN (Local Area Network) and someone is currently connected to your computer, Windows 95 displays a warning dialog box indicating that you're about to disconnect one or more people.

✦ Choose OK to go ahead and make these folks mad as all get out.

✦ Otherwise, choose Cancel and then find out who's connected and make it his or her responsibility to shut Windows 95 down on your computer after he or she logs off (so that you can go home and get a life).

If you ever restart the computer in MS-DOS mode, you can return to the comfort of Windows 95 by typing **exit** at the DOS prompt.

For more on shutting down your computer, see *Windows 95 For Dummies,* Chapter 5.

Starting Programs

In Windows 95, you can open your programs from the Start menu by double-clicking a program shortcut or program icon or by double-clicking an icon for a file created with the program.

How do I do it?

The most straightforward way to start a program in Windows 95 is from the Start menu. To do so, you follow these steps:

1. Click [Start] on the taskbar.

2. Choose [Programs ▶] on the Start menu to open a continuation menu listing all the programs installed on your computer.

3. Choose the program item you want to open on the Programs continuation menu. If the program has its own continuation menu (indicated by the arrowhead pointing to the right), choose the specific program item you want to open from this continuation menu.

4. Click the program item if you dragged your way through the menus without holding down the mouse button. Otherwise, release that mouse button you've been holding down so desperately as you've dragged over and down and up and then over and on and on and on to finally highlight that program item.

For pre-Windows 95 users only

In Windows 3.1 and earlier, you usually start your programs from the Program Manager by opening their group window and then double-clicking the program icon. When you install Windows 95 on your computer, it converts all your group windows to items on the Programs continuation menu. In turn, these items have their own continuation menus, where you find the command equivalents of the program icons that used to appear in the group window.

When do I do it?

Open a program from the Start menu (as I just described) when you don't routinely use the program and it's really too much trouble to go find one of its file icons or the actual program icon itself.

Open a program with a shortcut (either to the program or to a document you open regularly) when using that program is one of your main reasons for turning on the computer in the first place.

Open a program with a file when it's conveniently located or you had to locate the file with the Find feature or verify its contents with Quick View.

More stuff

See also "Shortcuts," in Part II, for information about creating ,shortcuts for opening a program or a file that in turn opens its program.

See also "Start Menu," in Part II, for information about manually adding items or removing them from the Programs continuation menu on the Start menu.

See also "File" in Part II and/or "Opening Files and Folders," in this part, for information about opening a program by opening its file.

See also "Getting a Quick View of a File's Contents," in this part, for information about peeking inside a file before you open it to determine if it's really the one you want to open after all.

See also "Finding Files and Folders," in this part, for information about searching for files in Windows 95.

Switching between Programs

The Windows 95 taskbar makes switching between programs as easy as clicking the button representing the program's window.

How do I do it?

To activate a program and bring it to the top of the pile, simply click the program's button on the taskbar.

Isn't there another way?

Windows old-timers can still use the Alt+Tab shortcut keys first introduced in Windows 3.0 to switch among all open windows. In Windows 95, however, you see a dialog box (like the one shown following) with icons for each program window (and a description) when you hold down the Alt key as you press Tab. When you let up on both the Alt and Tab keys, Windows activates the window for whatever program icon is selected (by being enclosed in a box).

> Microsoft Word - Document1

When do I do it?

Switch to another program that you have open anytime you need to check something in that program or get some work done. You also need to switch to a program so that you can close its window (and thereby shut it down) when you no longer need its services but do need the computer memory that the program is hogging.

More stuff

See also "Taskbar," in Part II, for more on doing tricks with the amazing taskbar.

Uninstalling Programs

Windows 95 includes an uninstall utility that takes the pain out of removing unneeded or obsolete versions of a program from your computer.

How do I do it?

To uninstall a program installed with Windows 95 (**see** "Installing Programs" earlier in this part), you follow these steps:

1. Click ⊞Start on the taskbar.

2. Choose 🔩 Settings ▸ on the Start menu.

3. Choose 🖾 Control Panel ↘ from the Settings continuation menu to open the Control Panel window.

Add/Remove
Programs

4. Double-click Add/Remove Programs in the Control Panel to open the Add/Remove Programs Properties dialog box.

5. Select the program to be removed in the list box in the Install/ Uninstall tab of the Add/Remove Programs Properties dialog box, and then select the Remove button.

When do I do it?

Use the Windows 95 uninstaller to get rid of any unwanted program that you've installed with the Add/Remove Control Panel. Using this utility to remove a program (rather than just deleting the program's folder) ensures that all vestiges of the program are removed from the system and that you get back every byte of storage space that you're entitled to.

More stuff

See also "Add/Remove Programs," in Part V, for more on installing and removing programs in Windows.

Part IV

Accessories for Every Appetite

The accessories are the extra little programs thrown into the Windows 95 operating system for good measure. This part of the book contains an alphabetical listing of all the accessory programs from Calculator to WordPad. Here, you find out how to do fun stuff like the things mentioned in the following list.

In this part . . .

✔ Use the Calculator accessory to find out just how broke you are

✔ Use the Character Map accessory to insert all sorts of weird symbols into your e-mail

✔ Use the Games accessory to lighten up and have a little fun in life

✔ Use the Multimedia accessory to play your favorite Madonna CD

✔ Use the Phone Dialer accessory to call home and explain why you'll be late for the fifth time this week

. . . and much, much more.

Remember: If you find that some of the accessories covered in this part of the book are not on your computer, you can use the Add/Remove Programs control panel to add some of them (see "Add/Remove Programs" in Part 5 for details on opening this control panel).

Arranging the Icons in a Window

Along with everyday stuff like My Computer and the Explorer, Windows 95 offers a bunch of smaller accessory programs (known officially as *accessories*). Some of these accessories, like the Calculator, WinPad, and Games, you may use day in and day out (well, at least the Games). Others, like the Fax Viewer, Dial-Up Networking, and HyperTerminal, you may use rarely, if ever.

If you find that some of the accessories covered in this section were not installed on your computer as part of the Windows 95 installation, you can use the Add/Remove Programs control panel to add some of them (*see* "Control Panel" in Part II for details on opening this control panel). Follow these steps:

1. Choose the Windows Setup tab in the Add/Remove Programs Properties dialog box.

2. Select Accessories at the top of the list box in the Add/ Remove Programs Properties dialog box.

3. Click the Details button to open the Accessories dialog box.

The Accessories dialog box shows you which accessories are currently installed on your computer with check marks next to their names in its list box.

4. To add any of the uninstalled accessories (those without check marks), click its check box to add a check mark to it.

5. When you're finished specifying the accessories to add, choose OK twice: first to close the Accessories dialog box and then a second time to close the Add/Remove Programs Properties dialog box.

Make sure that you have your Windows 95 program disks or CD-ROM handy so that you can supply the necessary files to Windows (it prompts you for whatever disk is required). After adding the accessories, you have to restart Windows 95 before they appear on the Accessories menu.

Calculator

The Calculator accessory supplies you with an on-screen calculator that you can use to perform all sorts of arithmetic computations on the fly.

How do I get to it?

To open the Calculator accessory, follow these steps:

1. Click 🏁 Start on the taskbar.

2. Choose 📇 Programs ▶ on the Start menu.

3. Choose 📁 Accessories ▶ at the top of the Programs continuation menu.

4. Choose 🖩 Calculator near the top of the Accessories continuation menu.

Calculator					
Edit View Help					

		Back	CE	C

MC	7	8	9	/	sqrt
MR	4	5	6	*	%
MS	1	2	3	-	1/x
M+	0	+/-	.	+	=

What do I do with it?

The calculator works just like those cheap battery- and solar-powered ones that you use to balance your checkbook:

✦ To enter a value, click the number buttons or type the number in from the top row or numeric keypad.

✦ To clear an entry, click the CE button.

✦ To clear the calculator of all entries and calculations, click the C button.

✦ To add one value to another, enter the first value, click the + button, enter the second value, and then click the = button.

✦ To subtract one value from another, enter the first value, click the – button, enter the second value, and then click the = button.

✦ To multiply one value by another, enter the first value, click the * button, enter the second value, and then click the = button.

✦ To divide one value by another, enter the first value, click the / button, enter the second value, and then click the = button.

✦ To get the square root of a value, enter the value and then click the sqrt button.

✦ To store a value or the result of a calculation into the calculator's memory, enter the value or perform the calculation and then click the MS button.

✦ To add a value or calculation to those already stored in the calculator's memory, enter the value or perform the calculation and then click the M+ button.

✦ To enter a value stored in the calculator's memory, click the MR button.

✦ To clear the calculator's memory, click the MC button.

If you're an engineer and need access to enigmatic functions such as sine, cosine, and tangent, you can switch the simple bank-balance version of the calculator to a fancy-Dan scientific calculator (shown in the following figure) by choosing Scientific from the View pull-down menu.

More stuff

See also "Accessories," at the beginning of Part II, for general information on the accessories in Windows 95.

Calendar

The Calendar accessory gives you an on-screen appointment book.

Remember: This accessory is only available if you've installed Windows 95 over a previous version of Windows 3.1.

How do I get to it?

To open the Calendar accessory, you follow these steps:

1. Click ▓Start on the taskbar.

2. Choose ▓▓ Programs ▶ on the Start menu.

3. Choose ▓▓ Accessories ▶ at the top of the Programs continuation menu.

4. Choose ▓▓ Calendar on the Accessories continuation menu.

What do I do with it?

You can use the Calendar to record and review all your important appointments for the day (such as lunch with Princess Di at 12:30 and interview for better job at 3:00). You can even set an alarm to remind you of particularly important moments that you don't want to miss in your day (like break time, lunch time, and quitting time!).

More stuff

See also "Accessories" at the beginning of Part II for general information on the accessories in Windows 95.

Cardfile

This accessory lets you create and maintain an on-screen version of a cardfile. Not only can you keep names, addresses, and phone numbers of your coworkers and clients but you can also record comments about them (like who still owes you five bucks).

Remember: This accessory is only available if you've installed Windows 95 over a previous version of Windows 3.1.

How do I get to it?

To open the Cardfile accessory, you follow these steps:

1. Click **Start** on the taskbar.

2. Choose **Programs** ▸ on the Start menu.

3. Choose **Accessories** ▸ at the top of the Programs continuation menu.

4. Choose **Cardfile** on the Accessories continuation menu.

What do I do with it?

The Cardfile accessory lets you search for specific cards by any word in that card as well as list all the cards in order by any line of the card you wish. If you have a modem in your computer, you can also use an autodial feature to have Windows 95 dial the phone number shown in the card. (You simply put the insertion point on the line of the card containing the phone number and then press F5 or choose Autodial on the Card pull-down menu.)

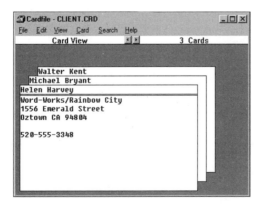

Note that Cardfile works in Windows 95 just like it did in earlier versions of Windows. In fact, Cardfile shows just how far behind the times it is by not even accepting long filenames, a telltale sign that the program hasn't been updated for Windows 95 (see "Long Filenames" in Part II). This means that if you insist on using Cardfile to maintain your names and addresses, you must still assign those stupid eight-dot-three filenames (with the program automatically suggesting .crd as the three character file extension) to the files that hold your cards.

More stuff

See also "Accessories," at the beginning of Part II, for general information on the accessories in Windows 95.

Character Map

The Character Map accessory lets you copy any character in a particular font (including the weird ones that you can't insert directly from the keyboard) into the Clipboard. From there, you can insert it into any kind of text file you may be working on.

How do I get to it?

To open the Character Map accessory, follow these steps:

1. Click ▦ Start on the taskbar.

2. Choose ▦ Programs ▸ on the Start menu.

3. Choose ▦ Accessories ▸ at the top of the Programs continuation menu.

4. Choose ▦ Character Map on the Accessories continuation menu.

What do I do with it?

To copy characters in and out of the Clipboard with the Character Map accessory, follow these steps:

1. Choose the font containing the character(s) you want to copy in the Font drop-down list box of the Character Map dialog box.

2. Pick the characters in the selected font that you want to copy to the Clipboard by double-clicking them or clicking them and then choosing the Select button (to display a larger version of a particular character, keep the mouse button pressed after clicking it).

3. Choose the Copy button to actually copy the selected characters (now proudly displayed in the Characters to copy edit box) to the Clipboard.

4. Switch to the program containing the open text file where you want the copied characters to appear (*see* "Switching between Programs" in Part III of this book if you've never done this before).

5. Position the insertion point at the place in the document text where the copied characters are to be inserted and then choose Paste from the Edit pull-down menu or press Ctrl+V.

Keep in mind that the document text into which you insert the copied characters must be in the same font that was originally selected when you copied the characters with the Character Map accessory. This means that if you copy some cute graphic characters like the telephone and floppy disk from the Wingdings font into the Clipboard with Character Map and then insert them into a WordPad document (*see* "WordPad" in this part for information about using this word processor) using the Times New Roman font, you end up with "(<" where the cute little telephone and floppy disk should be!

More stuff

See also "Accessories," at the beginning of Part II, for general information on the accessories in Windows 95.

Clipboard Viewer

The Clipboard Viewer accessory lets you see what has been placed in the Clipboard with either the Cut or Copy command on the Edit pull-down menu.

How do I get to it?

To use the Clipboard Viewer accessory, follow these steps:

1. Click **Start** on the taskbar.

2. Choose **Programs** on the Start menu.

3. Choose **Accessories** at the top of the <u>P</u>rograms continuation menu.

4. Choose **Clipboard Viewer** on the Accessories continuation menu.

What do I do with it?

You can use the Clipboard Viewer to make sure that the Clipboard contains exactly the stuff that you want before you go ahead and actually paste the stuff into one or more of your documents.

Remember: The Clipboard is the special place in your computer's memory that holds whatever data you select and put there with either the Cu<u>t</u> or <u>C</u>opy command on the <u>E</u>dit pull-down menu (or with the keyboard shortcuts Ctrl+X or Ctrl+C, respectively). You can insert the contents of the Clipboard into any Windows document by positioning the insertion point at the place where the stuff should appear and then choosing the <u>P</u>aste command on the <u>E</u>dit menu (or by pressing Ctrl+V).

Keep in mind that the Clipboard holds only the stuff you last put there with the Cu<u>t</u> or <u>C</u>opy command, meaning that if you copy some text from a WordPad document into the Clipboard and then switch over to the Paint accessory, and there copy a picture from one of its documents into the Clipboard, the Clipboard will contain only the Paint graphic (having wiped out the WordPad text to accommodate the Paint picture).

To preview the current contents of the Clipboard before you paste its stuff into your document, simply open the Clipboard Viewer accessory (as outlined in the preceding section).

You can cut or copy text, graphics, or even entire files or folders into the Clipboard with the Cu<u>t</u> and <u>C</u>opy commands on the <u>E</u>dit menu.

+ If you copy text (be it words or numerical data) to the Clipboard, the text appears in the Clipboard Viewer more or less as entered (except that columns may no longer line up).

+ If you copy a graphic image, the Clipboard Viewer shows the image more or less as it was drawn.

+ If, however, you copy a file or folder into the Clipboard, the Clipboard Viewer shows only the file's or folder's path and filename. For example, if you copy into the Clipboard a file named Sales Summary for 1995 that's been saved in a folder named Sales Stuff on your hard disk, you see

C:\SALES STUFF\SALES SUMMARY FOR 1995

at the top of the Clipboard Viewer window when you open the Clipboard Viewer accessory.

More stuff

See also "Accessories," at the beginning of Part II, for general information about the accessories in Windows 95.

Dial-Up Networking

The Dial-Up Networking accessory is the kind of thing you use when you have a desktop computer at home or a laptop computer on the road that's networked together with your work computer and want to access your e-mail and/or use other files on your main PC at work via your modem.

How do I get to it?

To use the Dial-Up Networking accessory, follow these steps:

1. Click 🏁 Start on the taskbar.

2. Choose 📁 Programs ▶ on the Start menu.

3. Choose 📁 Accessories ▶ at the top of the Programs continuation menu.

4. Choose 📁 Dial-Up Networking on the Accessories continuation menu.

```
┌─────────────────────────────────┐
│ 📁 Dial-Up Networking   _ □ ✕   │
│ File  Edit  View  Connections   │
│ Help                            │
│   ┌──┐        ┌──┐              │
│   │📠│        │📠│              │
│   └──┘        └──┘              │
│  Make New     San Fran          │
│  Connection   Office            │
│                                 │
│                                 │
│ 2 object(s)                     │
└─────────────────────────────────┘
```

What do I do with it?

The first time you select the Dial-Up Networking accessory, Windows starts a Welcome to Dial-Up Networking Wizard that walks you through the steps for setting up your computer either so that it can dial into other computers or so that others can dial into it. After that initial use, you can create additional dial-up connections for other computers with this accessory either by double-clicking the Make New Connection icon in the Dial-Up Networking dialog box or by choosing the Make New Connection command from the Connections pull-down menu.

When you set up your computer so that it can dial up another computer, you create a connection that contains information about the type of modem on your computer and the name and telephone number of the computer you're connecting to. You can then use this connection to dial up the other computer by double-clicking its icon in the Dial-Up Networking dialog box and then choosing the Connect button in the Connect To dialog box.

More stuff

See also "Accessories," at the beginning of Part II, for general information on the accessories in Windows 95.

Direct Cable Connection

You use the Direct Cable Connection accessory when you need to connect two computers that are located in the same place but aren't already networked. For example, you can use this accessory to connect a laptop computer to your desktop PC and then copy the data files from the PC to the laptop that you need to take with you on a business trip.

How do I get to it?

To use the Direct Cable Connection accessory, follow these steps:

1. Click 🪟 Start on the taskbar.

2. Choose 📁 Programs ▶ on the Start menu.

3. Choose 📁 Accessories ▶ at the top of the Programs continuation menu.

4. Choose 🔗 Direct Cable Connection on the Accessories continuation menu to open the Direct Cable Connection Wizard.

What do I do with it?

In order to successfully set up a connection between two computers with the Direct Cable Connection accessory, you need a parallel or serial cable (parallel is faster, if you have it) that reaches between the two machines. If you have a parallel cable, you connect the ends of it to the ports marked LPT1 on the backs of both computers. If you have a serial cable, connect the ends of it to the ports marked either COM1 or COM2 on the backs of both computers (don't you dare connect one end to COM1 and the other to COM2!).

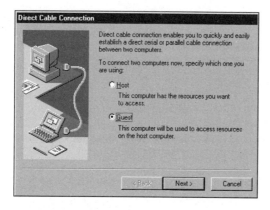

When you select the Direct Cable Connection accessory, Windows
starts the Direct Cable Connection Wizard that walks you through
the steps for connecting two computers.

✦ If you run this accessory on the computer that contains the
data you want to copy to the other, you choose the Host radio
button option in the first screen of the Direct Cable Connection Wizard.

✦ If you're running the accessory on the computer to which you
want to copy data files, you choose the Guest radio button on
this screen instead.

After you choose the Next> button in this Wizard, you need to
select the type of cable and port connection (Parallel cable on
LPT1, Serial cable on COM1, or Serial cable).

After selecting the type of connection and port, you can then
physically connect the cable to the selected type of port on each
computer.

After you select the Finish button to close the Direct Cable
Connection Wizard, you then need to select the same Direct Cable
Connection accessory on the other computer, this time specifying
the opposite setting (meaning that you choose Guest if you
previously chose Host or you choose Host if you previously chose
Guest).

More stuff

For general information on the accessories in Windows 95, see
"Accessories" at the beginning of Part II.

Fax

The Fax accessory lets you compose a new fax, design a new cover page with the Cover Page Editor, or retrieve a file from a fax service via your modem.

How do I get to it?

To open the Fax accessory, follow these steps:

1. Click 🏁Start on the taskbar.
2. Choose 🔳 Programs ▶ on the Start menu.
3. Choose 📁 Accessories ▶ at the top of the Programs continuation menu.
4. Choose 📁 Fax ▶ on the Accessories continuation menu.
5. Choose Compose New Fax, Cover Page Editor, or Request a Fax on the Fax continuation menu.

What do I do with it?

Use Compose New Fax when you want to send a fax to someone and don't care about the formatting and fonts used in the message part of the fax (if you do care about this stuff, you need to send the fax via the New Message command on the Compose menu in the Microsoft Exchange — *see* "Microsoft Exchange" in Part II for details).

Use the Cover Page Editor to design a new cover page to use with the faxes you send.

Use Request a Fax to retrieve a document from a fax information service via the Retrieve a specific document from the Request a Fax Wizard.

Compose New Fax

Choosing the Compose New Fax command from the Fax continuation menu opens the Compose New Fax Wizard that you can use to send a fax via the modem connected to your computer. Follow these steps:

1. If necessary, change the dialing properties for your location (such as the access number to get out of the building, if you have call waiting, that sort of thing). Do this by choosing the

Dialing Properties button in the first page of the Compose New Fax Wizard before you click the Next> button or press Enter to go on to the second page.

2. On the second page, type the name of the fax recipient in the To edit box. Next, type in the fax number of your recipient in the Fax # area code and telephone number edit boxes and check the Dial area code check box if you are calling an area other than your own. If the fax number you're dialing doesn't require a long distance country code (such as 1 for the US), be sure that you choose the (None - internal extension) option in the Country code drop-down list box.

If the recipient of the fax is in your Personal Address Book, you can select his or her name by clicking the Address Book button. Designate the name or names of the recipients in the Address Book dialog box by selecting the name in the left-hand list box. Then click the To-> button to copy the name to the right-hand Message Recipients list box. If you select more than one name, Windows will separate each name. When you finish selecting the recipients' names, choose OK or press Enter. The selected names will appear in the Recipients: list box when you return to the Compose New Fax Wizard.

3. Press the Next> button to go to the third page of the Wizard where you can indicate whether you want a cover page. You can also select a new cover page style (created with the Cover Page Editor — see "Fax Cover Page Editor" in the next section) from the list box. Choose the Options button to change fax settings such as message formats, when to send the faxes, and what billling code to use.

4. When you've got the recipients and faxing options all set, choose the Next> button to go to the fourth page of the Wizard where you can compose your fax. Type your Subject and Note in the appropriate boxes.

5. Choose the Next> button to go to the fifth page of the Wizard, which allows you to choose one or more files to send along with your fax. To select a file to include, choose the Add File button and then select the file in the Open a File to Attach dialog box. After selecting the filename, click the Open button or press Enter to close the Open a File to Attach dialog box and return to the Compose New Fax Wizard. The path and filename of the file you selected will now appear in the Files to send list box.

6. Choose the Next> button to go to the sixth and final page of the Wizard where you can choose the Finish button and press Enter to send the fax.

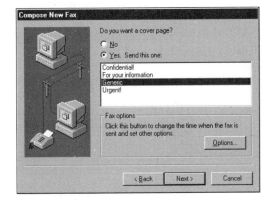

Compose New Fax

To: Melinda Bryant   Address Book...

Country: United States of America (1)

Fax #: (415) 555-4567   ☐ Dial area code

⇩ Add to List

Recipient list:

Remove

< Back   Next >   Cancel

Compose New Fax

Do you want a cover page?

◯ No

⦿ Yes. Send this one:

Confidential!
For your information
Generic
Urgent!

Fax options

Click this button to change the time when the fax is sent and set other options.

Options...

< Back   Next >   Cancel

Compose New Fax

Subject:

Party Line Rumor Alert

Note:

Beware the Ides of March!

☑ Start note on cover page

< Back   Next >   Cancel

Fax Cover Page Editor

The fax cover page that you design with the Fax Cover Page Editor can include the company logo or other appropriate artwork. You can also define specific fields on the cover page to contain certain types of information, such as your name and fax number along with the recipient's name and fax number.

TIP

The easiest way to create a new fax cover page is to open one of the existing templates supplied with Windows 95: Choose the Open command from the File pull-down menu. You can choose from four templates: Confidential, For your information, General purpose, and Urgent! (all these files are located in the Windows folder on your hard disk). You can then modify this basic fax cover page template as your needs require and save the changes under a different filename with the Save As command on the File pull-down menu.

In the following figure, you can see the top part of the General purpose fax cover page after opening this fax form template in the Fax Cover Page Editor in a maximized window.

Retrieve File

Choosing Retrieve File from the Fax continuation menu opens the Retrieve File from a Fax Service Wizard that you can use to retrieve a document sent to a fax information service via the modem connected to your computer. You can choose between retrieving whatever files are available at the fax service or retrieving a specific file. After deciding this, you have to specify only the name and telephone number of the service and indicate whether you want to call as soon as possible, when the telephone rates are discounted, or at a specific time.

More stuff

See also "Accessories," at the beginning of Part II, for general information on the accessories in Windows 95.

See also "Microsoft Exchange," in Part II, for information on sending faxes with the Microsoft Exchange.

Fax Viewer

The Fax Viewer accessory lets you improve the display of the contents of a fax received via a fax/modem connected to your computer.

How do I get to it?

To open the Fax Viewer, follow these steps:

1. Click ![Start] on the taskbar.

2. Choose ![Programs] on the Start menu.

3. Choose ![Accessories] at the top of the Programs continuation menu.

4. Choose ![Fax Viewer] on the Accessories continuation menu.

What do I do with it?

A fax received via a fax/modem can be one of two kinds: *editable* (meaning that the fax was sent from another computer and was formatted with some kind of program like Word or WordPad that your system can understand) or *noneditable* (meaning that the fax was sent from a stand-alone modem and was not formatted with a program that your system can interpret — in fact, its text could well be handwritten and/or contain printed graphics and text composed who-knows-where). You only need to use the Fax Viewer to open and read the latter type of noneditable faxes, as editable faxes automatically open the program they were formatted with when you open them.

To improve the legibility of a fax opened in the Fax Viewer:

✦ Use the <u>R</u>otate menu commands if you need to set the fax right-side up.

✦ Use the <u>Z</u>oom menu commands if you need to either zoom in or zoom out in order to read its contents. Keep in mind that changing the zoom of a fax on your screen has no effect on its proportions should you print the fax with the <u>P</u>rint command on the <u>F</u>ile pull-down menu.

More stuff

See also "Accessories," at the beginning of Part II, for general information on the accessories in Windows 95.

See also "Microsoft Exchange," in Part II, for information on faxes with the Microsoft Exchange.

Games

Since all work and no play makes you a very dull employee, Windows 95 includes several games to help you while away the hours.

How do I get to it?

To play one of the Games accessories, follow these steps:

1. Click **Start** on the taskbar.

2. Choose **Programs** on the Start menu.

3. Choose **Accessories** at the top of the Programs continuation menu.

4. Choose **Games** at the top of the Accessories continuation menu.

5. Choose the game you want to play (FreeCell, Hearts, Minesweeper, or Solitaire) on the Games continuation menu.

In the following figure, you can see that I just lost a tough game of Minesweeper by landing on a bomb.

In the next figure, you can see that I'm just getting ready to play a fierce game of Hearts with my good pals Bear, Michele, and Bunny.

What do I do with it?

The Games accessories let you play any of the following games:

✦ FreeCell is a card game that is a lot like the Solitaire game included in earlier versions of Windows; it differs from Solitaire in that all the cards in FreeCell are always face up.

✦ Hearts is a great version of the card game we all know and love.

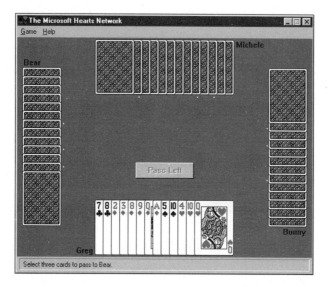

 ✦ Minesweeper is the same game of marking mines that Microsoft gave you in earlier versions of Windows.

✦ Solitaire is the old standby game of Solitaire first included in Windows 3.0 and 3.1.

TIP

If you need information about how to play the game that you've opened, choose <u>C</u>ontents from the <u>H</u>elp pull-down menu located on the game's menu bar.

More stuff

TIP

If your computer is part of a Local Area Network you can play Hearts with your coworkers on the network. To do so, choose the I want to <u>c</u>onnect to another game radio button in the Microsoft Hearts Network dialog box that appears when you start the Hearts game.

See also "Accessories," at the beginning of Part II, for general information on the accessories in Windows 95.

HyperTerminal

The HyperTerminal accessory is the kind of thing you use when you have a desktop computer at home or a laptop computer on the road that is not networked to your computer at the office, but you still want to be able to send and receive files between the computer at home or the laptop on the road and the computer in your office via your modem.

How do I get to it?

To use the HyperTerminal accessory to communicate with another computer by modem, follow these steps:

1. Click [Start] on the taskbar.

2. Choose [Programs ▶] on the Start menu.

3. Choose [Accessories ▶] at the top of the Programs continuation menu.

4. Choose [HyperTerminal] on the Accessories continuation menu.

What do I do with it?

Selecting this accessory opens the HyperTerminal window, which contains the Hypertrm icon along with icons for other e-mail services like CompuServe, AT&T, and MCI Mail. When you double-click the Hypertrm icon, a Connection Description dialog box opens, prompting you to enter a description for the new connection you are creating, select an icon for it, indicate the telephone number to which the computer's modem is connected, and indicate the port you are connecting to on the remote computer. To connect to the remote computer, simply choose the Dial button in the Connect dialog box that comes up at the end of this process.

After creating a connection, you can use it by double-clicking its icon in the HyperTerminal window and then choosing the Dial button in the Connect dialog box that appears or by selecting the icon in the HyperTerminal window and then choosing the Dial command from the File pull-down menu.

You can also dial up a connection after opening a particular HyperTerminal connection in its own window by choosing the Connect command from the Call pull-down menu or by clicking the Connect button (the picture of the telephone with the receiver down) on the window's toolbar.

After connecting to the remote computer, you can send files by using the menus or the toolbar: Choose either the Send File or Send Text File command on the Transfer pull-down menu or, on the toolbar, click the Send button (the picture of a piece of paper with little dots in front of it, indicating that it's moving from one place to another) and indicate the file to send. Likewise, you can receive a file that's being sent to you from the remote computer by choosing Receive File on the Transfer menu or by clicking the Receive button (the picture of a piece of paper sticking out of a folder with the downward-pointing arrow above it) on the toolbar.

When you're finished transferring files between the connected computers, you can terminate the connection and free up the telephone line by choosing Disconnect from the Call menu or by clicking on the Disconnect button (the picture of a telephone with the receiver about to crash down on it) on the toolbar.

More stuff

See also "Accessories," at the beginning of Part II, for general information on the accessories in Windows 95.

Multimedia

The Multimedia accessories include a bunch of useful multimedia utilities (useful, that is, if your computer is equipped with a CD-ROM drive, a sound card, external speakers, and a microphone).

How do I get to it?

To use one of the Multimedia accessories, follow these steps:

1. Click  on the taskbar.

2. Choose ![Programs] on the Start menu.

3. Choose ![Accessories] at the top of the Programs continuation menu.

4. Choose ![Multimedia] near the top of the Accessories continuation menu.

5. Choose the Multimedia utility that you want to use (CD Player, Media Player, Sound Recorder, or Volume Control) on the Multimedia continuation menu.

In the following figure, you see the Media Player accessory after I opened Microsoft's sample digital movie (called SAMPLE.AVI). After playing a little bit of the movie, I stopped the movie on a frame that has this hotdog skier stuck in mid-air.

In the next figure, you see the CD Player accessory after I popped in my favorite Meat Loaf CD and started listening to Track 2 ("Life Is a Lemon and I Want My Money Back").

What do I do with it?

The Multimedia accessories include the following:

✦ **CD Player** lets you play an audio CD (compact disc) in your computer's CD-ROM drive.

✦ **Media Player** lets you play a digital movie or sound file on your computer.

✦ **Sound Recorder** lets you record on disk with a microphone connected to your sound card.

✦ **Volume Control** lets you set the volume and balance for your speakers when playing audio CDs or system sounds or when recording with your microphone.

More stuff

See also "Accessories," at the beginning of Part II, for general information on the accessories in Windows 95.

See also "Multimedia," in Part V, for information on changing different multimedia settings for your computer.

Notepad

The Notepad accessory offers a simple editor that you can use to read, edit, and print simple text files (such as those last-minute README files that seem to accompany all your software programs).

How do I get to it?

To open the Notepad accessory, follow these steps:

1. Click  on the taskbar.

2. Choose [Programs ▶] on the Start menu.

3. Choose [Accessories ▶] at the top of the Programs continuation menu.

4. Choose [Notepad] on the Accessories continuation menu.

In this figure, you see the Notepad accessory after I started composing a very important memo.

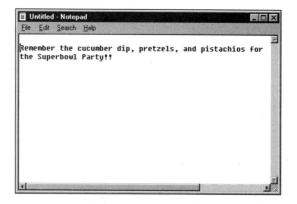

What do I do with it?

Text files composed in Notepad use a standard, bold Arial font with very simple formatting (there is no way to change fonts or attributes or automatically center, any of that good stuff, in Notepad). Use Notepad to compose files whenever you know that the document must be saved in a true ASCII-type text file or whenever you're not sure that the recipient's computer is equipped with a word processor capable of opening and reading a file that's been truly word-processed, such as Word or WordPad (see "WordPad" later in this part).

To compose a new text file in Notepad, open the program and start typing your heart out. When you come to the end of a line and need to start a new line or a new paragraph, be sure to press the Enter key. Notepad is not your typical word processor; if you don't press Enter to start a new line, it just keeps on going, and going, and going. . . . Notepad does this because it is first and foremost a text editor for editing programming files where carriage returns signify a new line of code.

To open a text file after starting Notepad, choose Open on the File pull-down menu and designate the name of the text file to open. By default, Notepad looks only for files that use the .txt filename extension. To display all the files in the current folder (shown in the Look in edit box at the top of the Open dialog box), choose All Files (*.*) in the Files of type drop-down list box. When you've located the text file to open, select its file icon and then choose the Open button or double-click it to open the text file in Notepad.

To save a new text file or the changes you've made to the text file you just opened, choose the Save command from the File pull-down menu. If you're saving a text file for the first time, type its new name in the File name edit box of the Save As dialog box before you press Enter or choose the Save button.

When a file sports the spiral-bound notebook icon, you can tell that it has been saved as a Notepad file and will automatically open Notepad if you double-click it.

More stuff

See also "Accessories," at the beginning of Part II, for general information on the accessories in Windows 95.

Paint

The Paint accessory offers a simple drawing program with which you can create original graphics or edit bitmapped graphics that you get with Windows 95 or other Windows-based programs.

How do I get to it?

To open the Paint accessory, follow these steps:

1. Click ▓Start on the taskbar.

2. Choose ▓ Programs ▸ on the Start menu.

3. Choose ▓ Accessories ▸ at the top of the Programs continuation menu.

4. Choose ▓ Paint on the Accessories continuation menu.

In the following figure, you see the Paint accessory after I used it to whip up a self-portrait.

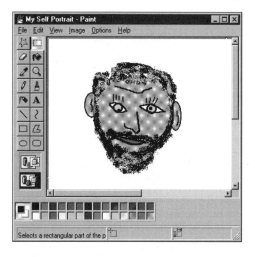

What do I do with it?

When you select the Paint accessory, Windows opens an empty Paint window that contains a palette of artist tools on the left side and a palette of colors to choose from on the bottom.

To open a bitmap file with an existing graphic to edit, choose Open from the File pull-down menu and then designate the filename. To create your own original masterpiece, select a drawing tool and have at it!

You can use the Paint accessory to create your own wallpaper designs for the desktop. Just follow these simple steps:

1. After you finish drawing a new graphic or editing an existing one, save it with the Save or Save As command on the File menu.

If necessary, give your new creation a filename.

2. Choose the Set As Wallpaper (Tiled) or the Set As Wallpaper (Centered) command from the File menu (choose Tiled if you're working with a less-than-full-screen picture and want Windows to replicate it so that it fills the entire screen).

As soon as you select one of these Set As Wallpaper commands, Windows 95 immediately makes your wonderful artwork the backdrop against which all further Windows actions take place.

More stuff

See also "Accessories," at the beginning of Part II, for general information on the accessories in Windows 95.

Phone Dialer

The Phone Dialer accessory lets you call all your friends and family from your computer via your modem (even if they aren't in your calling circle).

How do I get to it?

To open the Phone Dialer accessory, follow these steps:

1. Click **Start** on the taskbar.

2. Choose **Programs** on the Start menu.

3. Choose **Accessories** at the top of the Programs continuation menu.

4. Choose **Phone Dialer** on the Accessories continuation menu.

What do I do with it?

When you select this accessory, Windows 95 opens the Phone Dialer window, where you can specify the number to call and have your computer dial it.

The Phone Dialer contains a neat speed-dial feature that stores up to eight telephone numbers (entered in the Edit Speed Dial dialog box that you access by choosing Speed Dial from the Edit pull-down menu). You can dial a number stored on a speed dial button simply by clicking its button (or pressing Alt plus its speed dial number). In addition to using the speed dial buttons to enter the phone number to call, you can enter the telephone number in the Number to dial edit box by clicking the digits on the ten-key pad.

One of the great features of the Phone Dialer accessory is that you can specify all the dialing parameters required by your telephone system (done from the Dialing Properties dialog box opened by choosing Dialing Properties from the Tools pull-down menu). These calling parameters can include stuff like the codes for making outside local calls, codes for making long-distance calls, and even which calling card to use in making toll calls.

More stuff

See also "Accessories," at the beginning of Part II, for general information on the accessories in Windows 95.

System Tools

The System Tools accessories comprise a bunch of utilities for keeping your computer system in tip-top shape.

How do I get to it?

To use one of the System Tools accessories, follow these steps:

1. Click 🏁Start on the taskbar.

2. Choose 📁 Programs ▶ on the Start menu.

3. Choose ▣ Accessories ▶ at the top of the Programs continuation menu.

4. Choose ▣ System Tools ▶ near the top of the Accessories continuation menu.

5. Choose the particular System Tools accessory (Backup, Disk Defragmenter, DriveSpace, Inbox Repair Tool, Net Watcher, Resource Meter, ScanDisk, or System Monitor) that you want to open on the System Tools continuation menu.

What do I do with it?

The System Tools accessories include a number of powerful utilities that can go a long way toward letting you spend quality time with your computer:

✦ **Backup** lets you make, compare, or restore backup copies of particular files and folders on either floppy disks or tape. Use this utility to maintain copies of all the files you can't live without in case (knock on wood) anything ever happens to your computer or its hard disk.

✦ **Disk Defragmenter** defragments your hard disk, which means that your files are rearranged so that they use contiguous blocks. This process usually speeds up your computer considerably and is necessary if you use the Media Player (*see* "Multimedia" earlier in this part).

✦ **DriveSpace** compresses your hard disk files to increase storage space.

✦ **Inbox Repair Tool** lets Windows scan and, if necessary, repair damaged or unreadable files that you receive via the Microsoft Exchange.

✦ **Net Watcher** lets you view all the connections currently made to your computer on the LAN (Local Area Network) as well as add or stop sharing folders with other users on the network.

✦ **Resource Meter** monitors the system resources used by the various programs that you are currently running. Note that using this accessory can make your computer run more slowly.

✦ **ScanDisk** checks your floppy disks or hard disk for errors and, if possible, fixes the errors that it finds.

✦ **System Monitor** lets you view all kinds of charts that plot various aspects of the computer system's performance. You can chart data for all sorts of junk you probably couldn't care

less about, such as Kernal Threads, the number of IPX packets lost per second, and the percentage of Dirty Data in the 32-bit file system.

More stuff

The Preview version of Windows 95 contains a WinBug command at the very bottom of the System Tools continuation menu that you can use to file an official Windows 95 bug report with Microsoft (via CompuServe). Don't use this command unless you are sure that you are experiencing a real Windows bug and not trying to get the operating system to do something it just wasn't designed to do.

See also "Accessories," at the beginning of Part II, for general information on the acccessories in Windows 95.

WinPopup

WinPopup lets you know when you receive new e-mail messages from others on your network and lets you send quickie e-mail messages to them.

How do I get to it?

Normally, once you've installed the WinPopup accessory, its dialog box automatically appears each time you start or log onto your computer. If you don't want the WinPopup dialog box automatically "popping up" in your face every time you start the computer, you need to remove the WinPopup shortcut from the Startup folder (***see*** "Start Menu" in Part II) and move this shortcut to the desktop. From then on, you'll have to double-click the WinPopup shortcut icon on the desktop if you want to open the WinPopup dialog box.

WinPopup	
Messages Help	
No messages	
Current message: 0	Total number of messages: 0

What do I do with it?

WinPopup provides a quick and dirty way to exchange messages with other people on your network. Normally when you receive a message from somone, WinPopup lets you know by playing a sound (using its Options, you can also have its dialog box automatically pop up when a message comes in). To read the message you have only to open the WinPopup dialog box by clicking its button on the taskbar.

If you've got a bunch of messages, you can peruse them by clicking the Next and Previous buttons (Next has two arrowheads pointing right while Previous has two pointing left). Each message you see in the WinPopup dialog box indicates the name of the sender as well as the date and time the message was sent.

If you see a message that you no longer need, you can get rid of it by clicking the Delete button (the one with the paper going into the trash can icon). Note, however, that all messages are automatically deleted as soon as you close the WinPopup dialog box or log off your computer.

To send a message to someone on the network, you follow these steps:

1. Open the WinPopup dialog box by clicking its button on the Start menu.

2. Click the Send button in the WinPopup dialog box or choose Send on the Messages pull-down menu (or press Ctrl+S) to open the Send Message dialog box.

3. In the To edit box, enter the name of the user or computer you want to send your message to.

To send the message to everyone in your workgroup, choose the Workgroup radio button to have Windows fill in the name of your workgroup in this edit box.

4. Type your message in the Message list box.

5. Choose OK or press the Enter key to send your message.

That's all there is to it! When Windows finishes sending your message, you get an alert box saying, "The message was successfully sent."

More stuff

See also "Start Menu," in Part II, for information on adding and removing shortcuts to the Startup folder.

WordPad

WordPad is a kind of "poor man's Microsoft Word," offering you basic document editing and formatting capabilities and compatibility with documents created with the real Microsoft Word.

How do I get to it?

To open the WordPad accessory and take a letter, follow these steps:

1. Click  on the taskbar.

2. Choose [Programs] on the Start menu.

3. Choose [Accessories] at the top of the Programs continuation menu.

4. Choose [WordPad] at the bottom of the Accessories continuation menu.

In the following figure, you see the WordPad accessory after I started using it to write my new novel, Alice in Windows™land.

What do I do with it?

Although it's not nearly as full-featured as Microsoft Word, WordPad's certainly head and shoulders above the NotePad text editor, as it lets you change fonts and attributes and format the text with justification or bullets. In fact, WordPad is so sophisticated that you can even preview how pages in the document will print. You access this print preview feature by choosing Print Preview from the File menu (or clicking the Print Preview button on the toolbar — the one with the magnifying glass).

Note that WordPad automatically saves its documents in the Word 6 file format, meaning that Word 6 can open any document created with WordPad. Likewise, WordPad can open any document created in Word 6. If you double-click a document in a folder or on the desktop that was created in WordPad but saved in the Word 6 file format, Windows 95 naturally tries to open Microsoft Word rather than the WordPad accessory, provided that Word 6 is installed on your computer.

If your computer is connected to a network, you can easily send copies of the documents you create and edit in WordPad to your coworkers on the network simply by choosing Send from the WordPad File pull-down menu. Doing so opens the Microsoft Exchange window with a blank message form, where you specify the recipients for the WordPad document and send documents to them.

More stuff

See also "Accessories," at the beginning of Part II, for general information on the accessories in Windows 95.

See also "Microsoft Exchange," in Part II, for specific information on sending messages on a network via the Microsoft Exchange.

Part V

Control Panel City

The control panels in Windows 95 are the place to go when you need to make changes to various settings for your computer system. In this part of the book, you find out how to do great stuff like the things mentioned in the following list:

In this part . . .

- ✔ Use the Date and Time control panel to correct the time on your computer so that you're not always late for every meeting.

- ✔ Use the Display control panel to mess with your windows color scheme and switch the wallpaper to something truly horrendous like Triangles!

- ✔ Use the Keyboard control panel to make your cursor blink faster.

- ✔ Use the Mouse control panel to soup up your double-clicks.

- ✔ Use the System control panel to finally find out just what kind of a computer the boss palmed off on you anyway!

. . . and much, much more.

Accessibility Options

The Accessibility Options control panel lets you change a number of keyboard, sound, display, and mouse settings that can make using the computer easier if you have less than perfect physical dexterity.

How do I get to it?

To open the Accessibility Options control panel, follow these steps:

1. Click ⊞Start on the taskbar.

2. Choose 🔣 Settings ▸ on the Start menu.

3. Choose 🖳 Control Panel on the Settings continuation menu.

Accessibility
Options

4. Double-click the Accessibility Options icon in the Control Panel window.

Accessibility Properties ?✕

Keyboard | Sound | Display | Mouse | General

─ StickyKeys ────────────────────────────
Use StickyKeys if you want to use Shift, Ctrl, or Alt key by pressing one key at a time.

☐ Use StickyKeys   Settings...

─ FilterKeys ────────────────────────────
Use FilterKeys if you want Windows to ignore brief or repeated keystrokes, or slow the repeat rate.

☐ Use FilterKeys   Settings...

─ ToggleKeys ────────────────────────────
Use ToggleKeys if you want to hear tones when pressing Caps Lock, Num Lock, and Scroll Lock.

☐ Use ToggleKeys   Settings...

☐ Show extra keyboard help in programs

OK | Cancel | Apply

What do I do with it?

When you double-click the Accessibility Options icon in the Control Panel window, you get the Accessibilities Properties dialog box (isn't that a mouthful?) that contains the following tabs:

✦ **Keyboard tab:** Enable or disable StickyKeys, FilterKeys, and ToggleKeys.

- *StickyKeys* lets you use shortcuts that combine Shift, Ctrl, or Alt with some other key by pressing one key at a time (instead of both keys simultaneously as is usually the case).

- *FilterKeys* slows the repeat rate or has Windows ignore repeated keystrokes (you can change this in the Settings for FilterKeys dialog box accessed with the Settings button on the Keyboard tab).

- *ToggleKeys* has Windows 95 play tones when you engage the Caps Lock, Num Lock, or Scroll Lock key.

✦ **Sound tab:** Enable or disable SoundSentry and ShowSounds if you're hearing impaired. SoundSentry generates a visual warning when Windows 95 makes some kind of warning sound. ShowSounds has your applications display captions for any sounds that they make.

✦ **Display tab:** Turn on or off High Contrast. High Contrast selects a high contrast color scheme (Blue and Black by default, although you can change this in the Settings for High Contrast dialog box accessed with the Settings button on the Display tab) and large lettering for the window's title and menu bar to make the screen easier to read if you're visually impaired.

✦ **Mouse tab:** Enable or disable MouseKeys. MouseKeys lets you control the mouse pointer with the keys on your computer's numeric keypad.

✦ **General tab:** Turn on or off Automatic reset, Notification, and SerialKey devices.

- *Automatic reset* can apply your accessibility changes to the current Windows session only or reset these features after the computer is idle for a set number of minutes (five minutes by default).

- *Notification* gives you an audible warning when an accessibility feature is turned on or off.

- *SerialKey devices* enable alternate input devices connected to your computer (via the serial port COM1, although you can change this in the Settings for SerialKey dialog box accessed with the Settings button on the General tab).

More stuff

See also "Control Panels," in Part II, for general information on control panels in Windows 95.

Add New Hardware

The Add New Hardware control panel is just the thing for installing new hardware devices for your computer.

How do I get to it?

To open the Add New Hardware control panel, follow these steps:

1. Click [Start] on the taskbar.

2. Choose [Settings] on the Start menu.

3. Choose [Control Panel] on the Settings continuation menu.

4. Double-click the Add New Hardware icon in the Control Panel window.

Add New
Hardware

What do I do with it?

The Add New Hardware Wizard that opens when you select the Add New Hardware icon walks you through the installation of some new piece of hardware such as a new sound card or CD-ROM player. Just be aware that this old Wizard asks you a whole bunch of technical questions about the hardware you're installing. If you're not prepared to supply all the answers, you'd do best to leave this operation to someone more computer-savvy (that way, you can blame that person if the installation gets messed up).

More stuff

See also "Control Panels," in Part II, for general information on control panels in Windows 95.

Add/Remove Programs

The Add/Remove Programs control panel lets you install or uninstall programs on your computer.

How do I get to it?

To open the Add/Remove Programs control panel, follow these steps:

1. Click [Start] on the taskbar.

2. Choose [Settings ▶] on the Start menu.

3. Choose [Control Panel] on the Settings continuation menu.

Add/Remove
Programs

4. Double-click the Add/Remove Programs icon in the Control Panel window.

What do I do with it?

When you double-click the Add/Remove Programs icon on the Control Panel, you get the Add/Remove Programs Properties dialog box, which lets you both install and (yeah!) uninstall applications (that is, programs) on your computer. You can also use its Windows Setup tab to remove from your computer various accessories (*see* Part IV) and sundry objects that you don't use, a step that you may need to take when disk space is at a premium. Finally, you can use its Startup Disk tab to create a floppy disk with which you can start your computer in an emergency — should Windows 95 go sour on you for some unexplainable reason, for example.

Add/Remove Programs Properties   [?] [X]

Install/Uninstall | Windows Setup | Startup Disk |

To install a new program from a floppy disk or CD-ROM drive, click Install.

[Install...]

The following software can be automatically removed by Windows. To remove a program, select it from the list and click Remove.

[Remove...]

[OK] [Cancel] [Apply]

Creating a start-up disk

I urge each and every one of you to take the time to create such a start-up disk so that you have some way to get your computer going should, heaven forbid, Windows 95 freak out on you.

To make a start-up disk, you follow these simple steps in the Add/ Remove Programs Properties dialog box:

1. Click the Startup Disk tab.

2. Find a blank floppy disk (it doesn't have to be formatted).

3. Find your Windows 95 disks marked Disk 1 and Disk 2.

4. Insert the Windows 95 Disk 1 into your floppy drive.

5. Click the Create Disk button in the Startup Disk tab of the Add/ Remove Programs Properties dialog box.

6. Replace the Windows 95 Disk 1 with Disk 2 and click OK when prompted to do so.

7. When prompted, insert your blank floppy — the one that you clearly labeled "Windows 95 Startup Disk" — in drive A (this may or may not be the one that contains your Windows 95 Disk 2) and click OK when prompted to do so. If the disk isn't already formatted, a new dialog box telling you that Windows must format the disk will appear. You must choose its OK button to have Windows format the disk before copying the start-up info onto the disk.

Add/Remove Programs Properties ? ✕

Install/Uninstall | Windows Setup | Startup Disk

If you have trouble starting Windows, you can use a startup disk to start your computer, run diagnostic programs, and fix any problems. To create a startup disk, click Create Disk. You will need one floppy disk.

Create Disk...

OK | Cancel | Apply

After Windows 95 finishes copying information to your Windows 95 start-up disk, you can close the Add/Remove Programs Properties dialog box and remove the start-up disk. Be sure to store your Windows 95 disks and your new start-up disk in a safe place (but not so safe that you forget where in the blazes you put them should the need for them someday arise).

More stuff

You can install new Windows 95-based programs on your computer in the same way you do under Windows 3.0 and 3.1: with the Run command on the File menu in the Program Manager. However, because Windows 95 no longer uses the Program Manager, if you want to use the Run command, you have to go through the Start menu to open the Run dialog box, where you enter the program's installation command (usually a:\install or a:\setup).

If you're installing older applications (called 16-bit apps by the techies), use the Run command to install them, because doing so will match more closely their installation instructions. However, new Windows 95 applications (called 32-bit apps by the techies) will probably be easier to install with the Install/Uninstall tab of the Add/Remove Programs Properties dialog box (especially if the software is being installed from a CD-ROM rather than floppy disks).

For more on using the Run command, *see* "Start Menu" in Part II. For specific instructions on installing programs with Add/Remove Programs in the Control Panel, *see* "Installing Programs" in Part III. For instructions on removing programs with Add/Remove Programs in the Control Panel, *see* "Uninstalling Programs" in Part III.

See also "Control Panels," in Part II, for general information on control panels in Windows 95.

Date/Time

The Date/Time control panel lets you reset the current date and time if either one ever gets out of whack (if you live in a region that goes in and out of daylight saving time, you have to change the time at least twice a year).

How do I get to it?

To open the Date/Time control panel, follow these steps:

1. Click 🔲 Start on the taskbar.

2. Choose 🖫 Settings ▶ on the Start menu.

3. Choose 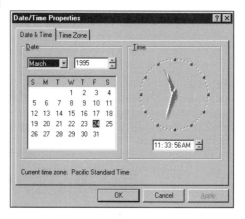 Control Panel on the <u>S</u>ettings continuation menu.

4. Double-click the Date/Time icon in the Control Panel window.

What do I do with it?

When you double-click the Date/Time icon in the Control Panel, you get the Date/Time Properties dialog box, which enables you to change the current date and time. You can also use the Time Zone tab in this dialog box to modify the time zone (by selecting the zone from the drop-down list box on the Time Zone tab) and indicate whether this number should be adjusted for daylight saving time.

You can always check your computer's clock by looking at the time displayed on the far right of the taskbar. If you need to adjust the way the date and time are formatted in Windows 95, you need to do so in the Regional Settings Properties dialog box (*see* "Regional Settings" later in this part).

More stuff

See also "Control Panels," in Part II, for general information on control panels in Windows 95.

Display

The Display control panel lets you fool around with the background, color schemes, and wallpaper used by Windows. This control panel also lets you select and turn on and off a screen saver to prevent your beautiful display from being burned into your monitor for all eternity!

How do I get to it?

To open the Display control panel, follow these steps:

Display

1. Click [Start] on the taskbar.

2. Choose [Settings] on the Start menu.

3. Choose [Control Panel] on the Settings continuation menu.

4. Double-click the Display icon in the Control Panel window.

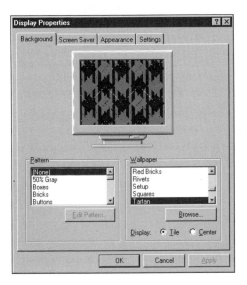

What do I do with it?

When you double-click the Display icon in the Control Panel, you get the Display Properties dialog box. Use the four tabs in that dialog box to change the following display settings:

◆ **Background tab:** Change the pattern or wallpaper used by the desktop (you change the color of the desktop with the Appearance tab, described in this list).

◆ **Screen Saver tab:** Select a screen saver and set the interval after which it kicks in. If you have one of those new energy-saving monitors, you can set the interval after which the monitor goes to lower-power standby or shuts off. (If you have such a monitor but Windows 95 isn't utilizing its energy-saving features, choose the Change Display Type button on the Settings tab and check the Monitor is Energy Star Compliant check box in the Change Display Type dialog box.)

✦ **Appearance tab:** Change the color scheme used by various parts of a window (*see* "Windows" in Part II for the lowdown on the parts) and/or the color of the desktop. If you change the appearance of an item that uses a font (such as the Icon Title, Inactive Title Bar, or Tooltip), you can change the font and its color, size, and attributes as well.

✦ **Settings tab:** Change the color palette (meaning the number of colors, such as 16, 256, or even, with some really fancy cards and monitors, millions) used by Windows 95 and resize the desktop area (the higher the number of pixels you select, the smaller the items and fonts appear on the desktop, although making them smaller does allow you to cram more stuff on-screen).

You can also use this tab to specify the kind of monitor you have if Windows 95 did not pick up on the monitor type when you first installed it or if you happen to have lucked out and scored a new monitor since Windows 95 was installed.

More stuff

See also "Control Panels," in Part II, for general information on control panels in Windows 95.

Find Fast

The Find Fast control panel lets you create and update various indexes that greatly speed up the file searches using specific text or phrases that you perform in Windows 95 or with a Microsoft Office 95 program (like Word 95 or Excel 95).

How do I get to it?

To open the Find Fast control panel, follow these steps:

1. Click ▓▓Start on the taskbar.

2. Choose ▓ Settings ▶ on the Start menu.

3. Choose ▓ Control Panel ▶ on the Settings continuation menu.

4. Double-click ▓ Find Fast in the Control Panel window.

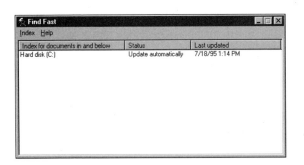

What do I do with it?

The Find Fast dialog box that opens when you select the Find Fast control panel shows you the indexes that have been created, their "update" status, and the date and time they were last updated. You can use this dialog box to either create a new index or update an existing one.

To create a new search index, you follow these steps:

1. Choose the Create Index command on the Index pull-down menu to open the Create Index dialog box.

2. Indicate the disk or folder for which the new index is being created in the In and below edit box. Use the Browse button to have Windows 95 supply this edit box with the path of the disk or folder that you select in the Find Fast Browse dialog box.

3. Select the type of files that should be covered in building the index in the Of type drop-down list box (Microsoft Office Documents is the default type but you can choose a specific type of Office document like Excel Workbooks or you can choose All Files if you want to include alien, non-Microsoft files).

4. Normally, Windows selects the Continue to update automatically check box so that your new index is updated automatically after you've edited or added files of the type on the disk or in the folder covered by the new index. Choose this check box to remove the check mark if you want to maintain control over when and if the index is updated (see the steps below on how to manually update an index).

5. Normally, Windows does not select the Speed up phrase searching check box. To have phrases included in the index to speed up your text searches even more, choose this check box to put a

checkmark in it (just be aware, as the note underneath says, that using this option makes the index a heck of a lot bigger than normal).

6. Choose the OK button or press Enter to have Windows 95 build the new index (and add it to the list in the Find Fast dialog box).

Create Index	? X

Index covers documents
In and below

[   ] Browse...

Of type

[Microsoft Office Documents]

☑ Continue to update automatically
☐ Speed up phrase searching
   (4 to 6 times more disk space is required for index)

[OK] [Cancel]

Note that if you create an index that is not continually updated automatically, you will want to manually update the index from time to time (especially after you've added a lot of documents of the type covered by the index). To manually update the index, follow these steps:

1. Select the index you want to update in the list box in the Find Fast dialog box.

2. Choose the Update Index command on the Index pull-down menu to open the Update Index dialog box.

3. Choose the OK button or press Enter in the Update Index dialog box to start the updating. If you want Windows to automatically update this index from then on, choose the Continue to update automatically check box before choosing OK in this dialog box.

More stuff

See also "Control Panels," in Part II, for general information on Control Panels in Windows 95.

See also "Finding Files and Folders," in Part III , for information how to search for files in Windows 95.

Fonts

The Fonts control panel lets you see all the wonderful fonts installed on your computer as well as install any new fonts you might get your hands on.

How do I get to it?

To open the Fonts control panel, follow these steps:

1. Click  on the taskbar.

2. Choose [🎛 Settings ▶] on the Start menu.

3. Choose [🔲 Control Panel] on the Settings continuation menu.

Fonts

4. Double-click the Fonts icon in the Control Panel window.

What do I do with it?

The Fonts window, which appears when you double-click the Fonts folder icon in the Control Panel, shows you all the fonts that are currently installed on your computer. Normally, the installed fonts appear as large icons in alphabetical order. You can, however, change how these fonts are displayed by selecting another setting from the View pull-down menu (List Fonts by Similarity is sometimes helpful in seeing just how many of your fonts look like a particular font such as Arial or Times New Roman, which are used pretty extensively in Windows 95).

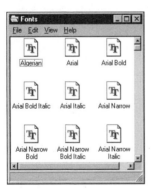

To see what a particular font looks like on-screen or in print, open the font either by double-clicking its icon in the Fonts window or by selecting its icon and then choosing Open from the File pull-down menu. Windows then opens a window just for that font that gives you its name, file size, version, and creator (or at least its copyright holder). Beneath this information, you find a sample of the font showing all the letters (in both lowercase and uppercase) followed by the numbers and punctuation symbols. Below this font sample, you find various type samples in 12, 18, 24, 36, 48, 60, and 72-point sizes.

To print the information and type samples for the font, choose the
<u>P</u>rint button in the upper-right corner of the font window. When
you're finished looking at the font, choose the <u>D</u>one button, opposite
the <u>P</u>rint button to the left, to close the specific font window and
return to the Fonts control window.

In addition to seeing which fonts are installed (something you can do
simply by opening a Font pull-down or drop-down menu in applications like Word or WordPerfect), you can also install and remove
fonts from the system in the Fonts window.

Adding and removing fonts

To add a new font, follow these steps:

1. Insert the disk or CD-ROM — whatever holds the fonts you want
to install — in your floppy or CD-ROM drive.

2. Choose <u>I</u>nstall New Font from the <u>F</u>ile pull-down menu of the
Fonts window to open the Add Fonts dialog box.

3. In the List of <u>F</u>onts list box, select the fonts that you want to
install. Then click OK or press Enter (if no fonts appear in the list
box, check that the correct drive and folder are selected in the
Dri<u>v</u>es and <u>D</u>irectories list boxes near the bottom of the Add
Fonts dialog box).

To remove a font from your computer, follow these steps:

1. In the Font window, select the icon for the font or fonts you want
to delete.

2. Press the Delete key or choose <u>D</u>elete from the <u>F</u>ile pull-down
menu.

3. Choose <u>Y</u>es to confirm the deletion of the font(s) in the Confirm
File Delete dialog box.

More stuff

Note that you can also drag the font icons to the Recycle Bin, which
allows you to delete them at some later time (*see* "Recycle Bin" in
Part II for details).

For general infomation on control panels in Windows 95, *see* "Control
Panels" in Part II.

Keyboard

The Keyboard control panel lets you fool around with stuff like the rate at which characters are repeated when you hold down a key and the country and language layout for the keyboard.

How do I get to it?

To open the Keyboard control panel, follow these steps:

1. Click 🚩Start on the taskbar.

2. Choose 🔧 Settings ▸ on the Start menu.

3. Choose 🖳 Control Panel ◥ on the Settings continuation menu.

Keyboard

4. Double-click the Keyboard icon in the Control Panel window.

What do I do with it?

The Keyboard Properties dialog box, which appears when you double-click the Keyboard icon in the Control Panel, contains the following three tabs for changing keyboard settings:

✦ **Speed tab:** Change the character repeat delay and rate as well as how fast the cursor blinks here.

✦ **Language tab:** Add keyboard layouts for languages other than the default of English, United States, and specify which keys to use to switch to a new keyboard layout (the Alt+Shift keys located on the left side of the keyboard or Ctrl+Shift) here.

✦ **General tab:** Change the type of keyboard used with your computer (you need to fool with this setting only if you get a new keyboard after installing Windows 95) here.

More stuff

See also "Control Panels," in Part II, for general information on control panels in Windows 95.

Mail and Fax

The Mail and Fax control panel lets you mess around with the information services that are at your fingertips when you use the Microsoft Exchange program.

How do I get to it?

To open the MS Exchange Settings Properties dialog box with the Mail and Fax control panel, follow these steps:

1. Click 🏁Start on the taskbar.

2. Choose 🖳 Settings ▶ on the Start menu.

3. Choose 🖾 Control Panel ▶ on the Settings continuation menu.

Mail and Fax

4. Double-click the Mail and Fax icon in the Control Panel window.

MS Exchange Settings Properties ✕

Services | Delivery | Addressing |

The following information services are set up in this profile:

Microsoft At Work Fax
Microsoft Mail
Personal Address Book
Personal Information Store

Add... | Remove | Properties |
Copy... | About... |

Show Profiles...

OK | Cancel | Apply | Help

What do I do with it?

The MS Exchange Settings Properties dialog box, which appears when you double-click the Mail and Fax icon on the Control Panel, lets you add, remove, or change the settings for the profiles required by Windows 95 to use various information services supported by the Microsoft Exchange program.

If you select the A̲dd button in the MS Exchange Settings Properties dialog box to add a new profile, Windows opens the Add Service to Profile dialog box where you can choose from available information services like Microsoft Network Online Service, Internet Mail, Microsoft Mail or Microsoft Fax.

More stuff

See also "Control Panels," in Part II, for general information on control panels in Windows 95.

See also "Microsoft Exchange," in Part II, for information on using the Microsoft Exchange.

Microsoft Mail Postoffice

The Microsoft Mail Postoffice control panel lets your network administrator administrate the workgroup postoffices for Microsoft Mail to his or her heart's content.

How do I get to it?

To open the Microsoft Mail Postoffice control panel, follow these steps.

1. Click [Start] on the taskbar.

2. Choose [Se̲ttings ▶] on the Start menu.

3. Choose [Control Panel] on the S̲ettings continuation menu.

4. Double-click the Microsoft Mail Postoffice icon in the Control Panel window.

Microsoft Mail
Postoffice

What do I do with it?

When you double-click the Microsoft Mail Postoffice icon in the Control Panel window, Windows 95 opens the Microsoft Workgroup Postoffice Admin Wizard, which walks you through the steps necessary for administrating an existing workgroup postoffice or creating a new one (in a workgroup postoffice, you can receive mail sent via Microsoft Mail in the Microsoft Exchange).

> **Microsoft Workgroup Postoffice Admin**   ✕
>
> Welcome to the Workgroup Postoffice Admin utility.
> Would you like to administer an existing workgroup
> postoffice, or create a new one?
>
> ⊙ Administer an existing Workgroup Postoffice
> ○ Create a new Workgroup Postoffice
>
> [< Back]   [Next >]   [Cancel]

More stuff

See also "Control Panels," in Part II, for general information on control panels in Windows 95.

See also "Microsoft Exchange," in Part II, for information on using the Microsoft Exchange.

Modems

The Modems control panel lets you install or remove a modem from your computer and get all kinds of technical gobbledygook about it (like its UART setting and ATI commands — yuck!).

How do I get to it?

To open the Modems control panel, follow these steps:

1. Click ▣Start on the taskbar.

2. Choose ▣ Settings ▶ on the Start menu.

3. Choose ▣ Control Panel ▶ on the Settings continuation menu.

Modems

4. Double-click the Modems icon in the Control Panel window.

What do I do with it?

The Modems Properties dialog box, which appears when you double-click the Modems icon in the Control Panel, lets you install a new modem, get information about the modems already installed on your computer, or remove installed modems from the system.

TIP

If something goes haywire with your modem and someone in technical support asks you which port the modem is connected to, you can find out by double-clicking Modems in the Control Panel window and then selecting the Diagnostics tab in the Modems Properties dialog box.

More stuff

See also "Control Panels," in Part II, for general information on control panels in Windows 95.

Mouse

The Mouse control panel lets you change all kinds of mouse settings, such as whether a right-handed or left-handed button configuration is used and the double-click speed.

How do I get to it?

To open the Mouse control panel, follow these steps:

1. Click 🪟Start on the taskbar.

2. Choose 🔧 Settings ▶ on the Start menu.

3. Choose 🖳 Control Panel on the Settings continuation menu.

4. Double-click the Mouse icon in the Control Panel window.

Mouse

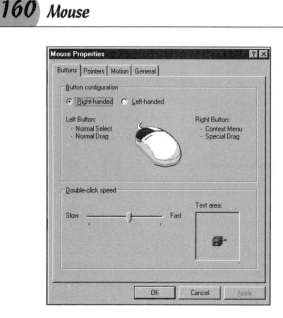

What do I do with it?

The Mouse Properties dialog box, which opens when you double-click the Mouse icon in the Control Panel, contains the following four tabs for changing settings for your mouse:

+ **Buttons tab:** Switch the primary and secondary buttons from right-handed to left-handed or back, or modify the double-click speed.

+ **Pointers tab:** Change which icon is used as the mouse pointer when you're doing different stuff in Windows, like selecting Help or selecting Text or when Windows is busy. To select a new icon for a function in Windows 95, you must have access to the file that contains the icon's graphic image.

+ **Motion tab:** Modify the speed of the mouse pointer and add or remove mouse trails (that mouse afterimage junk that will drive you nuts in no time at all).

+ **General tab:** Change the type of mouse connected to your computer (you need to use this one only if you get a new mouse after installing Windows 95).

More stuff

See also "Control Panels," in Part II, for general information on control panels in Windows 95.

Multimedia

The Multimedia control panel lets you mess with all sorts of multimedia settings, such as the playback or recording volume or recording quality for your sound card.

How do I get to it?

To open the Multimedia control panel, follow these steps:

1. Click **Start** on the taskbar.

2. Choose **Settings** ▸ on the Start menu.

3. Choose **Control Panel** on the Settings continuation menu.

4. Double-click the Multimedia icon in the Control Panel window.

Multimedia

What do I do with it?

The Multimedia Properties dialog box, which opens when you double-click the Multimedia icon in the Control Panel, contains the following five tabs for changing the settings involved with your multimedia enjoyment:

✦ **Audio tab:** Change the playback or recording volume level, the preferred device for recording, or the recording quality for your sound card.

✦ **MIDI tab:** Add MIDI instruments or select a custom configuration for music produced with MIDI.

✦ **CD Music tab:** Change the drive designation for the CD-ROM that contains the compact disc you want to listen to and change the volume setting when listening to the music through headphones (so that you don't disturb your coworkers or alert your boss to the fact that you're listening to Fleetwood Mac's Greatest Hits as you work).

✦ **Video tab:** Change the size of the window in which digital video plays on your computer.

✦ **Advanced tab:** Display all the multimedia devices currently installed on your computer and get information about particular devices (and possibly remove them).

![Multimedia Properties dialog box showing Audio tab with Playback and Recording settings]

More stuff

See also "Control Panels," in Part II, for general information on control panels in Windows 95.

Network

The Network control panel lets your network administrator administrate the LAN (Local Area Network) to his or her heart's content.

How do I get to it?

To open the Network control panel, follow these steps:

1. Click 📁Start on the taskbar.

2. Choose 🖥 Settings ▸ on the Start menu.

3. Choose 🖳 Control Panel ↘ on the Settings continuation menu.

Network

4. Double-click the Network icon in the Control Panel window.

Network	? X

Configuration | Identification | Access Control

The following network components are installed:

- Client for Microsoft Networks
- Client for NetWare Networks
- Dial-Up Adapter
- Intel EtherExpress 16 or 16TP
- IPX/SPX-compatible Protocol -> Dial-Up Adapter

[Add...] [Remove] [Properties...]

Primary Network Logon:

Client for NetWare Networks

[File and Print Sharing...]

Description

[OK] [Cancel]

What do I do with it?

The Network dialog box, which appears when you double-click the Network icon in the Control Panel, contains three tabs (Configuration, Identification, and Access Control) that enable your network administrator to modify a whole bunch of settings for your LAN (Local Area Network). These settings are not something that you should undertake unaided if you're a network lightweight, even if you consider yourself a Windows wonk.

More stuff

See Also "Control Panels," in Part II, for general information on control panels in Windows 95.

ODBC

The ODBC control panel lets you mess around with the data source drivers used in Windows 95.

How do I get to it?

To open the ODBC control panel, follow these steps:

1. Click [Start] on the taskbar.

2. Choose [Settings] on the Start menu.

3. Choose ▣ Control Panel ▶ on the <u>S</u>ettings continuation menu.

4. Double-click the ODBC icon in the Control Panel window.

What do I do with it?

The Data Sources dialog box, which opens when you double-click the ODBC (Open DataBase Connectivity) icon in the Control Panel, lets your database expert install new ODBC drivers or modify the settings for existing ODBC drivers. These drivers enable your system to access databases created with all kinds of weird database management software and let you add, delete, or configure the locations of those database files on your system (referred to as data sources).

More stuff

See also "Control Panels," in Part II, for general information on control panels in Windows 95.

Passwords

The Passwords control panel lets the network administrator for your LAN (Local Area Network) fool around with the passwords required to do various stuff in Windows 95.

How do I get to it?

To open the Passwords control panel, follow these steps:

1. Click 🚩Start on the taskbar.

2. Choose 🔧 <u>S</u>ettings ▶ on the Start menu.

3. Choose ▣ Control Panel ▶ on the <u>S</u>ettings continuation menu.

4. Double-click the Passwords icon in the Control Panel window.

What do I do with it?

The Passwords Properties dialog box, which opens when you double-click the Passwords icon in the Control Panel, contains three tabs for changing the security settings for your computer system:

✦ **Change Passwords tab:** Add or change the password required to use various services on your computer system (like Windows 95 itself).

+ **Remote Administration tab:** Enable remote administration of your computer and set (or change) the password that remote users must give in order to have access to your computer's files and printers.

+ **User Profiles tab:** Standardize all the preferences and desktop settings, or let individual users create their own profile settings, which determine what icons appear on the desktop and Start menu.

WARNING! Don't you dare fool around with these settings unless you're sure that you know what you're doing. The most ambitious thing you'd ever want to do with the Passwords Properties dialog box would be to reset a password for using Windows 95 or for accessing the stuff on your computer from a remote location. If you ever change your password, make sure that all the people who must have access to your data know what it is.

More stuff

See also "Control Panels," in Part II, for general information on control panels in Windows 95.

Printers

The Printers control panel shows you all the printers installed for use from your computer and lets you add new printers to the list.

How do I get to it?

To open the Printers control panel, follow these steps:

1. Click  on the taskbar.

2. Choose ▓ _Settings_ ▶ on the Start menu.

3. Choose ▓ _Control Panel_ ▶ on the <u>S</u>ettings continuation menu.

4. Double-click the Printers icon in the Control Panel window.

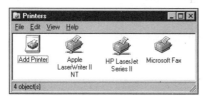

What do I do with it?

The Printers window, which opens when you double-click the Printers folder icon in the Control Panel, shows you all the printers that are currently installed for use on your computer (or your workgroup, if you are on a network) and lets you add a new printer.

Installing a new printer

To install a new printer in the Printers window, follow these steps:

1. Double-click the Add Printer icon in the Printers window to open the Add Printer Wizard.

2. Click Next> or press Enter.

3. Indicate whether the printer is a <u>L</u>ocal printer or <u>N</u>etwork printer by selecting the appropriate radio button; then choose Next> or press Enter.

4. Choose the printer's manufacturer in the <u>M</u>anufacturers list box; then choose the printer model in the <u>P</u>rinters list box.

5. If you have an installation disk for the printer you've selected, choose the Have <u>D</u>isk button, insert the disk in one of your floppy drives, and indicate the drive's location in the Manufacturer's information (located in the drop-down list box). Then choose OK or press Enter. If you don't have an installation disk for the printer you selected in Step 4, just choose the Next> button.

6. Select the port to which your new printer is connected in the Available Ports list box and then choose the Next> button. If you need to tweak the port settings (assuming that you know what you're doing), choose the Configure Port button and tweak away in the LPT such-and-such or COM such-and-such Properties dialog box.

7. Type the name you want associated with the new printer in the Printer name edit box and then choose the Next> button. If you want the new printer to become the default printer for all the printing you do in Windows 95, choose the Yes radio button before you choose the Next> button.

8. If you want to print a test page with your newly installed printer to make sure that it's properly installed, make sure that the Yes (recommended) radio button is selected under the text when you choose the Finish button or press Enter.

When you choose the Finish button, Windows copies the files it needs to install your printer. If you didn't indicate that you have an installation disk for the printer, you're prompted to insert one or more of your Windows 95 disks into your floppy drive and choose the OK button.

After copying the printer files, Windows 95 prints a test page using that printer (unless, of course, you choose the No radio button in Step 8). The test page shows the name and port connection of the printer along with some sample text. While this page is being printed, Windows 95 displays an alert box asking whether the page printed correctly. If you indicate yes, Windows congratulates you on a job well done. If you indicate no, Windows attempts to help you trouble-shoot the problem and tries to print the test page again.

Once a printer is installed, a printer icon with the printer's name appears in the Printers folder (if the printer is shared on a network, the printer icon has a line with a little yellow square, representing the network connection and cable, underneath the picture of the printer).

Using a printer's context menu

Each icon for nonshared printers has a context menu (if you don't know what the heck this is, please *see* "Context Menus" in Part II) that offers you the following commands:

✦ **Open** opens a window for that printer showing all the documents currently in its print queue (you can also do this by double-clicking the printer icon).

• If you want to remove a document from the queue, select it and then choose Cancel Printing from the Document pull-down menu.

- If you want to remove all the documents from the printer queue, choose Purge Print Jobs from the Printer menu.

- If you want to pause the printing, choose Pause Printing on the Document or Printer menu.

- If you want to move a job in the queue, drag it to its new position and then release the mouse button.

+ **Work Offline** enables you to send a document to a printer that is not currently connected to your computer (this command is available only on networked or laptop computers, which may not always have access to their printers).

  When you send a document to a printer when Work Offline has been selected (indicated by a check mark in front of the command name), Windows 95 stores the document until you choose this Work Offline command a second time (conceivably only after you've made sure that the printer is properly connected to your computer and ready to print).

+ **Set As Default** makes this printer the default printer automatically used by all Windows programs.

+ **Create Shortcut** creates a shortcut (if you don't know what this is, *see* "Shortcut" in Part II) for this printer on the desktop. After creating a shortcut for a printer, you can print a document that's been formatted for this printer simply by dragging the file and dropping it onto the printer shortcut on the desktop.

+ **Delete** uninstalls the printer.

+ **Rename** edits the name of the printer as it appears under its printer icon in the Printers window (you can also do so by clicking the I-beam mouse pointer somewhere in the name).

+ **Properties** displays or changes a bunch of settings for the printer, including things like which type of fonts to use (TrueType or PostScript), the resolution and halftone settings for printing graphics, and paper size, orientation, and type of feed.

You can also open the Printers folder by clicking the Start button and then selecting Settings on the Start menu and Printers on the Settings continuation menu.

You can open the window containing the print queue for a particular printer by clicking the printer icon displayed on the far right of the taskbar (right next to the speaker icon) with the secondary mouse button and then choosing the printer's name on the context menu that appears (this is equivalent to double-clicking a printer's icon in the Printers window or choosing Open on the printer's context menu as described in the preceding list).

More stuff

See also "Control Panels," in Part II, for general information on control panels in Windows 95.

Regional Settings

The Regional control panel lets you change the formatting for stuff like numbers, currency, dates, and times to suit schemes preferred by countries other than the U.S.

How do I get to it?

To open the Regional Settings control panel, follow these steps:

1. Click [Start] on the taskbar.

2. Choose [Settings] ▸ on the Start menu.

3. Choose [Control Panel] on the Settings continuation menu.

4. Double-click the Regional Settings icon in the Control Panel window.

Regional
Settings

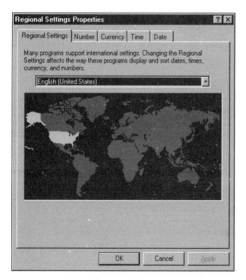

What do I do with it?

The Regional Settings Properties dialog box, which opens when you double-click the Regional Settings icon in the Control Panel, contains the following five tabs for changing settings affecting how programs display and sort numbers, currency, the time, and the date:

✦ **Regional Settings tab:** Select the language and country to be used as the basis for all regional settings.

✦ **Number tab:** Change the way numbers are formatted in programs.

✦ **Currency tab:** Change the way currency is formatted in programs.

✦ **Time tab:** Change the way times are formatted in programs.

✦ **Date tab:** Change the way dates are formatted in programs.

More stuff

See also "Control Panels," in Part II, for general information on control panels in Windows 95.

Sounds

In the Sounds control panel, you can mess around with assigning various sounds (like *Ding* and *Tada*) to common events, such as exiting Windows or opening a program window.

How do I get to it?

To open the Sounds control panel, follow these steps:

1. Click ⊞Start on the taskbar.

2. Choose ▓ Settings ▶ on the Start menu.

3. Choose 🖳 Control Panel ▶ on the Settings continuation menu.

Sounds

4. Double-click the Sounds icon in the Control Panel window.

What do I do with it?

The Sounds Properties dialog box, which opens when you double-click the Sounds icon in the Control Panel, lets you select various sound files to be played when certain events take place (for example, starting Windows 95, opening a new program, maximizing a window, or exiting Windows 95).

Assigning sounds to common events

To associate a cool sound with a particular event, follow these steps:

1. Select the event in the Events list box.

2. Select the sound file to be played in the Name drop-down list box.

> **Sounds Properties** [?] [×]
>
> Sounds
>
> Events:
> - **Windows**
>   - Asterisk
>   - Close program
>   - Critical Stop
>   - Default sound
>   - Exclamation
>   - Exit Windows
>   - Maximize
>
> Sound
> Name   Preview
> [None]   [▶] [■]
> [Browse...] [Details...]
>
> Schemes
> My Sound Settings
>   [Save As...] [Delete]
>
> [OK] [Cancel] [Apply]

3. To hear the sound, click the play button (the one with the right-pointing arrowhead right after the Preview loudspeaker icon).

4. To save all the sounds as currently configured with the Windows events, choose the Save As button and enter a descriptive name for the sound configuration, such as **A Little Windows 95 Light Music**.

More stuff

If you ever get tired of hearing Windows 95 beep, ding, and tada as you work, you can turn off all the sound by opening the Sounds Properties dialog box and selecting (None) in the Schemes drop-down list box.

Besides the boring old Chimes, Chord, Ding, and Tada that come with previous versions of Windows, Windows 95 ships with four different sound schemes (assuming that you installed all the Multimedia items when you installed Windows 95): Musica, Nature, Robotz, and Utopia. Each scheme has a bunch of different sounds that are already matched to specific Windows 95 events such as windows maximize, windows minimize, windows start, windows exit, and so on. You can select one of these ready-made schemes in the Schemes drop-down list box or mix and match sounds from different groups to create a custom scheme of your own.

For general infomation on control panels in Windows 95, *see* "Control Panels" in Part II.

System

The System control panel gives a whole bunch of technical information about your computer system (the most interesting of which are the name of the Intel processor and amount of RAM in your computer) as well as lets you modify a whole bunch of vital system settings (that you had best leave alone).

How do I get to it?

To open the System control panel, follow these steps:

1. Click 🏁 Start on the taskbar.

2. Choose 🔧 Settings ▸ on the Start menu.

3. Choose 💾 Control Panel ▸ on the Settings continuation menu.

System

4. Double-click the System icon in the Control Panel window.

What do I do with it?

The System Properties dialog box, which appears when you select the System icon in the Control Panel, lets you get system information about your computer as well as fool around with a lot of settings, such as removing devices (a definite no-no), setting up virtual memory (and if you don't know what that is, you don't need to be setting it) and specifying how much disk space to allocate to it, and optimizing the file systems (especially for use with older, 16-bit application programs).

If you're a lightweight in the Windows 95 department, you should open this dialog box for one purpose and one purpose only: namely, to find out what version of Windows 95 you're running, what type of computer you have (80386, 80486, or Pentium), and how much memory your computer's equipped with (you know, that RAM stuff). All this information is prominently displayed on the General tab on top of the System Properties dialog box (so there's no need to go messing with the Device Manager, Hardware Profiles, or Performance tabs that follow).

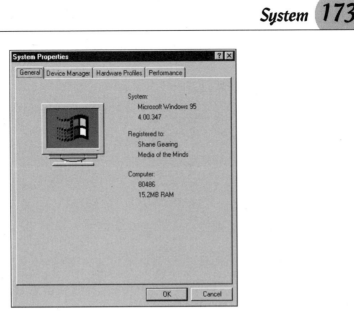

More stuff

See also "Control Panels," in Part II, for general information on control panels in Windows 95.

Techie Talk

accessories

Tiny (by Microsoft standards) auxiliary programs invented for Windows 95 that aren't really necessary to run your computer but can be really handy.

applications

A techie way of saying *programs,* you know, the things that make your computer run around the room and jump through hoops.

Clipboard

The place in your system memory where items you wish to cut or copy from one place to another are stored. The Clipboard only holds one item at a time and you can see the current Clipboard contents by using the Clipboard Viewer accessory.

context menu

A pull-down menu containing commands that relate directly to the object to which they are attached. Context or *shortcut* menus can be found almost everywhere in Windows 95. They're attached to program, folder, or file icons, toolbar buttons, open windows, and even the desktop itself. To open a context menu, you click the object in question with the secondary (that is, right, unless you're a lefty) mouse button.

control menu

A pull-down menu attached to every window in Windows 95 that contains the same old tired commands used to resize, relocate, or close the window just in case you can't adapt to the way Windows 95 performs these functions or you really miss this feature from Windows 3.1. The control menu appears as a small version of the program's icon in the top left corner of the program's window.

Control Panel

A window full of icons that let you customize the many Windows 95 settings available for your computer. Imagine that.

desktop

Well, it's not really a desktop, is it? No blotter board, overstuffed pen/pencil caddie, paper clip dispenser, family portraits, or anything. I mean, it may *sit* on your desktop but it's really your computer screen, the place where all the action is.

dialog box

A special limited type of window that contains any number of buttons, boxes, tabs, and sliders used to specify a whole bunch of settings all at once in Windows 95 or any other particular Windows program you have open.

DOS

An acronym for (choose one) Disk, Damned, Diabolical, Dumb (our favorite) Operating System. DOS is almost irrelevant with the advent of Windows 95. You can, however, open a window on DOS and have a look-see at your config.sys file within Windows 95 if you really miss that kind of stuff!

Explorer

A Windows 95 function that replaces the File Manager in our hearts and minds as the best way of viewing the folders, files, disk drives, CD-ROM drives, network drives, and who-knows-what-else that's part of your computer system.

filename

The name you give your files, silly. We're only bringing it up here because Windows 95 at long last allows the user to name their files and folders with up to 255 characters *including* spaces. Imagine that.

folder

A data container that holds files, other folders, or a combination of the two. Folders used to be called *directories* in Windows 3.1 even though their icons looked like folders. Windows 95 settles this confusion once and for all.

icon

A small picture used in Windows 95 to make your computer a more GUI (*gooey, as in Graphical User Interface*) place to be. Icons identify all manner of objects associated with your computer.

MSN / Microsoft Network

Allows all the users of Windows 95 to join together throughout the world in an atmosphere of Aquarian goodwill and brotherhood *or* just send and receive e-mail, get on-line help about Windows software, and participate in discussion forums. You can also access various services and, guess what? SURF THE NET!

properties

A description of the settings of any object in Windows 95 that is represented by an icon. Properties are found in special dialog boxes accessed through the object's context menu.

Recycle Bin

The trash can of Windows 95, where you can drag the files, directories, and other stuff that you want to get rid of. Somebody at Microsoft was positively gushing with political correctness when he named this thing since nobody is going to drive up, take the stuff you throw away, and make something wonderful and new with it.

shortcut

A remarkable way in Windows 95 to open a favorite document, folder, or program directly from the desktop of your computer without needing to know it's real whereabouts.

Start menu

The mother of all pull-down menus in Windows 95. Located by clicking the ever-present Start button on the taskbar, it contains almost all the commands you'll ever need to use.

taskbar

A bar that contains buttons for opening the Start menu and switching between programs and windows that are currently in use.

toolbar

A bar containing a row of buttons that perform many of the routine tasks you used to have to do with pull-down menus or keystroke combinations in Windows 3.1. Ubiquitous in Microsoft Office programs, they make their debut in Windows 95.

View menu

A new pull-down menu located in the menu bar that allows you to modify in various ways the look and feel of all those icons that are going forth and multiplying in your windows.

windows

The basic on-screen box used in Windows 95 to contain and display each and every program you run on your computer.

wizards

A particular set of dialog boxes used in Windows 95 and other Microsoft products to step the user through complex procedures like installing a new printer, sending a fax, or performing coronary angioplasty.

Index

Note: all italicized numbers indicate figure references.

E

F

(continued)

N

O

Notes

Notes

Notes

DUMMIES PRESS™

The Fun & Easy Way™ to learn about computers and more!

10/09/95

Windows® 3.11 For Dummies® 3rd Edition
by Andy Rathbone
ISBN: 1-56884-370-4
$16.95 USA/$22.95 Canada

Mutual Funds For Dummies™
by Eric Tyson
ISBN: 1-56884-226-0
$16.99 USA/$22.99 Canada

DOS For Dummies® 2nd Edition
by Dan Gookin
ISBN: 1-878058-75-4
$16.95 USA/$22.95 Canada

The Internet For Dummies® 2nd Edition
by John Levine & Carol Baroudi
ISBN: 1-56884-222-8
$19.99 USA/$26.99 Canada

Personal Finance For Dummies™
by Eric Tyson
ISBN: 1-56884-150-7
$16.95 USA/$22.95 Canada

PCs For Dummies® 3rd Edition
by Dan Gookin & Andy Rathbone
ISBN: 1-56884-904-4
$16.99 USA/$22.99 Canada

Macs® For Dummies® 3rd Edition
by David Pogue
ISBN: 1-56884-239-2
$19.99 USA/$26.99 Canada

The SAT® I For Dummies™
by Suzee Vlk
ISBN: 1-56884-213-9
$14.99 USA/$20.99 Canada

Here's a complete listing of IDG Books' ...For Dummies® titles

Title	Author	ISBN	Price
DATABASE			
Access 2 For Dummies®	by Scott Palmer	ISBN: 1-56884-090-X	$19.95 USA/$26.95 Canada
Access Programming For Dummies®	by Rob Krumm	ISBN: 1-56884-091-8	$19.95 USA/$26.95 Canada
Approach 3 For Windows® For Dummies®	by Doug Lowe	ISBN: 1-56884-233-3	$19.99 USA/$26.99 Canada
dBASE For DOS For Dummies®	by Scott Palmer & Michael Stabler	ISBN: 1-56884-188-4	$19.95 USA/$26.95 Canada
dBASE For Windows® For Dummies®	by Scott Palmer	ISBN: 1-56884-179-5	$19.95 USA/$26.95 Canada
dBASE 5 For Windows® Programming For Dummies®	by Ted Coombs & Jason Coombs	ISBN: 1-56884-215-5	$19.99 USA/$26.99 Canada
FoxPro 2.6 For Windows® For Dummies®	by John Kaufeld	ISBN: 1-56884-187-6	$19.95 USA/$26.95 Canada
Paradox 5 For Windows® For Dummies®	by John Kaufeld	ISBN: 1-56884-185-X	$19.95 USA/$26.95 Canada
DESKTOP PUBLISHING/ILLUSTRATION/GRAPHICS			
CorelDRAW! 5 For Dummies®	by Deke McClelland	ISBN: 1-56884-157-4	$19.95 USA/$26.95 Canada
CorelDRAW! For Dummies®	by Deke McClelland	ISBN: 1-56884-042-X	$19.95 USA/$26.95 Canada
Desktop Publishing & Design For Dummies®	by Roger C. Parker	ISBN: 1-56884-234-1	$19.99 USA/$26.99 Canada
Harvard Graphics 2 For Windows® For Dummies®	by Roger C. Parker	ISBN: 1-56884-092-6	$19.95 USA/$26.95 Canada
PageMaker 5 For Macs® For Dummies®	by Galen Gruman & Deke McClelland	ISBN: 1-56884-178-7	$19.95 USA/$26.95 Canada
PageMaker 5 For Windows® For Dummies®	by Deke McClelland & Galen Gruman	ISBN: 1-56884-160-4	$19.95 USA/$26.95 Canada
Photoshop 3 For Macs® For Dummies®	by Deke McClelland	ISBN: 1-56884-208-2	$19.99 USA/$26.99 Canada
QuarkXPress 3.3 For Dummies®	by Galen Gruman & Barbara Assadi	ISBN: 1-56884-217-1	$19.99 USA/$26.99 Canada
FINANCE/PERSONAL FINANCE/TEST TAKING REFERENCE			
Everyday Math For Dummies™	by Charles Seiter	ISBN: 1-56884-248-1	$14.99 USA/$22.99 Canada
Personal Finance For Dummies™ For Canadians	by Eric Tyson & Tony Martin	ISBN: 1-56884-378-X	$18.99 USA/$24.99 Canada
QuickBooks 3 For Dummies®	by Stephen L. Nelson	ISBN: 1-56884-227-9	$19.99 USA/$26.99 Canada
Quicken 8 For DOS For Dummies® 2nd Edition	by Stephen L. Nelson	ISBN: 1-56884-210-4	$19.95 USA/$26.95 Canada
Quicken 5 For Macs® For Dummies®	by Stephen L. Nelson	ISBN: 1-56884-211-2	$19.95 USA/$26.95 Canada
Quicken 4 For Windows® For Dummies® 2nd Edition	by Stephen L. Nelson	ISBN: 1-56884-209-0	$19.95 USA/$26.95 Canada
Taxes For Dummies™ 1995 Edition	by Eric Tyson & David J. Silverman	ISBN: 1-56884-220-1	$14.99 USA/$20.99 Canada
The GMAT® For Dummies™	by Suzee Vlk, Series Editor	ISBN: 1-56884-376-3	$14.99 USA/$20.99 Canada
The GRE® For Dummies™	by Suzee Vlk, Series Editor	ISBN: 1-56884-375-5	$14.99 USA/$20.99 Canada
Time Management For Dummies™	by Jeffrey J. Mayer	ISBN: 1-56884-360-7	$16.99 USA/$22.99 Canada
TurboTax For Windows® For Dummies®	by Gail A. Helsel, CPA	ISBN: 1-56884-228-7	$19.99 USA/$26.99 Canada
GROUPWARE/INTEGRATED			
ClarisWorks For Macs® For Dummies®	by Frank Higgins	ISBN: 1-56884-363-1	$19.99 USA/$26.99 Canada
Lotus Notes For Dummies®	by Pat Freeland & Stephen Londergan	ISBN: 1-56884-212-0	$19.95 USA/$26.95 Canada
Microsoft® Office 4 For Windows® For Dummies®	by Roger C. Parker	ISBN: 1-56884-183-3	$19.95 USA/$26.95 Canada
Microsoft® Works 3 For Windows® For Dummies®	by David C. Kay	ISBN: 1-56884-214-7	$19.99 USA/$26.99 Canada
SmartSuite 3 For Dummies®	by Jan Weingarten & John Weingarten	ISBN: 1-56884-367-4	$19.99 USA/$26.99 Canada
INTERNET/COMMUNICATIONS/NETWORKING			
America Online® For Dummies® 2nd Edition	by John Kaufeld	ISBN: 1-56884-933-8	$19.99 USA/$26.99 Canada
CompuServe For Dummies® 2nd Edition	by Wallace Wang	ISBN: 1-56884-937-0	$19.99 USA/$26.99 Canada
Modems For Dummies® 2nd Edition	by Tina Rathbone	ISBN: 1-56884-223-6	$19.99 USA/$26.99 Canada
MORE Internet For Dummies®	by John R. Levine & Margaret Levine Young	ISBN: 1-56884-164-7	$19.95 USA/$26.95 Canada
MORE Modems & On-line Services For Dummies®	by Tina Rathbone	ISBN: 1-56884-365-8	$19.99 USA/$26.99 Canada
Mosaic For Dummies® Windows Edition	by David Angell & Brent Heslop	ISBN: 1-56884-242-2	$19.99 USA/$26.99 Canada
NetWare For Dummies® 2nd Edition	by Ed Tittel, Deni Connor & Earl Follis	ISBN: 1-56884-369-0	$19.99 USA/$26.99 Canada
Networking For Dummies®	by Doug Lowe	ISBN: 1-56884-079-9	$19.95 USA/$26.95 Canada
PROCOMM PLUS 2 For Windows® For Dummies®	by Wallace Wang	ISBN: 1-56884-219-2	$19.99 USA/$26.99 Canada
TCP/IP For Dummies®	by Marshall Wilensky & Candace Leiden	ISBN: 1-56884-241-4	$19.99 USA/$26.99 Canada

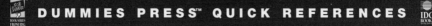

**The Internet For Macs®
For Dummies® Quick Reference**
by Charles Seiter

ISBN:1-56884-967-2
$9.99 USA/$12.99 Canada

**Windows® 95 For
Dummies® Quick Reference**
by Greg Harvey

ISBN: 1-56884-964-8
$9.99 USA/$12.99 Canada

**Photoshop 3 For Macs®
For Dummies® Quick Reference**
by Deke McClelland

ISBN: 1-56884-968-0
$9.99 USA/$12.99 Canada

**WordPerfect® For DOS
For Dummies® Quick Referen**
by Greg Harvey

ISBN: 1-56884-009-8
$8.95 USA/$12.95 Canada

Title	Author	ISBN	Price
DATABASE			
Access 2 For Dummies® Quick Reference	by Stuart J. Stuple	ISBN: 1-56884-167-1	$8.95 USA/$11.95 Cana
dBASE 5 For DOS For Dummies® Quick Reference	by Barrie Sosinsky	ISBN: 1-56884-954-0	$9.99 USA/$12.99 Cana
dBASE 5 For Windows® For Dummies® Quick Reference	by Stuart J. Stuple	ISBN: 1-56884-953-2	$9.99 USA/$12.99 Cana
Paradox 5 For Windows® For Dummies® Quick Reference	by Scott Palmer	ISBN: 1-56884-960-5	$9.99 USA/$12.99 Cana
DESKTOP PUBLISHING/ILLUSTRATION/GRAPHICS			
CorelDRAW! 5 For Dummies® Quick Reference	by Raymond E. Werner	ISBN: 1-56884-952-4	$9.99 USA/$12.99 Cana
Harvard Graphics For Windows® For Dummies® Quick Reference	by Raymond E. Werner	ISBN: 1-56884-962-1	$9.99 USA/$12.99 Cana
Photoshop 3 For Macs® For Dummies® Quick Reference	by Deke McClelland	ISBN: 1-56884-968-0	$9.99 USA/$12.99 Cana
FINANCE/PERSONAL FINANCE			
Quicken 4 For Windows® For Dummies® Quick Reference	by Stephen L. Nelson	ISBN: 1-56884-950-8	$9.99 USA/$12.95 Cana
GROUPWARE/INTEGRATED			
Microsoft® Office 4 For Windows® For Dummies® Quick Reference	by Doug Lowe	ISBN: 1-56884-958-3	$9.99 USA/$12.99 Cana
Microsoft® Works 3 For Windows® For Dummies® Quick Reference	by Michael Partington	ISBN: 1-56884-959-1	$9.99 USA/$12.99 Cana
INTERNET/COMMUNICATIONS/NETWORKING			
The Internet For Dummies® Quick Reference	by John R. Levine & Margaret Levine Young	ISBN: 1-56884-168-X	$8.95 USA/$11.95 Cana
MACINTOSH			
Macintosh® System 7.5 For Dummies® Quick Reference	by Stuart J. Stuple	ISBN: 1-56884-956-7	$9.99 USA/$12.99 Cana
OPERATING SYSTEMS:			
DOS			
DOS For Dummies® Quick Reference	by Greg Harvey	ISBN: 1-56884-007-1	$8.95 USA/$11.95 Cana
UNIX			
UNIX® For Dummies® Quick Reference	by John R. Levine & Margaret Levine Young	ISBN: 1-56884-094-2	$8.95 USA/$11.95 Cana
WINDOWS			
Windows® 3.1 For Dummies® Quick Reference, 2nd Edition	by Greg Harvey	ISBN: 1-56884-951-6	$8.95 USA/$11.95 Cana
PCs/HARDWARE			
Memory Management For Dummies® Quick Reference	by Doug Lowe	ISBN: 1-56884-362-3	$9.99 USA/$12.99 Cana
PRESENTATION/AUTOCAD			
AutoCAD For Dummies® Quick Reference	by Ellen Finkelstein	ISBN: 1-56884-198-1	$9.95 USA/$12.95 Cana
SPREADSHEET			
1-2-3 For Dummies® Quick Reference	by John Walkenbach	ISBN: 1-56884-027-6	$8.95 USA/$11.95 Cana
1-2-3 For Windows® 5 For Dummies® Quick Reference	by John Walkenbach	ISBN: 1-56884-957-5	$9.95 USA/$12.95 Cana
Excel For Windows® For Dummies® Quick Reference, 2nd Edition	by John Walkenbach	ISBN: 1-56884-096-9	$8.95 USA/$11.95 Cana
Quattro Pro 6 For Windows® For Dummies® Quick Reference	by Stuart J. Stuple	ISBN: 1-56884-172-8	$9.95 USA/$12.95 Cana
WORD PROCESSING			
Word For Windows® 6 For Dummies® Quick Reference	by George Lynch	ISBN: 1-56884-095-0	$8.95 USA/$11.95 Cana
Word For Windows® For Dummies® Quick Reference	by George Lynch	ISBN: 1-56884-029-2	$8.95 USA/$11.95 Cana
WordPerfect® 6.1 For Windows® For Dummies® Quick Reference, 2nd Edition	by Greg Harvey	ISBN: 1-56884-966-4	$9.99 USA/$12.99/Cana

DUMMIES PRESS™ QUICK REFERENCES

IDG BOOKS

Fun, Fast, & Cheap!™

10/09/95

**The Internet For Macs®
For Dummies® Quick Reference**
Charles Seiter

ISBN: 1-56884-967-2
$9.99 USA/$12.99 Canada

**Windows® 95 For
Dummies® Quick Reference**
by Greg Harvey

ISBN: 1-56884-964-8
$9.99 USA/$12.99 Canada

**Photoshop 3 For Macs®
For Dummies® Quick Reference**
by Deke McClelland

ISBN: 1-56884-968-0
$9.99 USA/$12.99 Canada

**WordPerfect® For DOS
For Dummies® Quick Reference**
by Greg Harvey

ISBN: 1-56884-009-8
$8.95 USA/$12.95 Canada

Title	Author	ISBN	Price
DATABASE			
Access 2 For Dummies® Quick Reference	by Stuart J. Stuple	ISBN: 1-56884-167-1	$8.95 USA/$11.95 Canada
dBASE 5 For DOS For Dummies® Quick Reference	by Barrie Sosinsky	ISBN: 1-56884-954-0	$9.99 USA/$12.99 Canada
dBASE 5 For Windows® For Dummies® Quick Reference	by Stuart J. Stuple	ISBN: 1-56884-953-2	$9.99 USA/$12.99 Canada
Paradox 5 For Windows® For Dummies® Quick Reference	by Scott Palmer	ISBN: 1-56884-960-5	$9.99 USA/$12.99 Canada
DESKTOP PUBLISHING/ILLUSTRATION/GRAPHICS			
CorelDRAW! 5 For Dummies® Quick Reference	by Raymond E. Werner	ISBN: 1-56884-952-4	$9.99 USA/$12.99 Canada
Harvard Graphics For Windows®			
For Dummies® Quick Reference	by Raymond E. Werner	ISBN: 1-56884-962-1	$9.99 USA/$12.99 Canada
Photoshop 3 For Macs® For Dummies® Quick Reference	by Deke McClelland	ISBN: 1-56884-968-0	$9.99 USA/$12.99 Canada
FINANCE/PERSONAL FINANCE			
Quicken 4 For Windows®			
For Dummies® Quick Reference	by Stephen L. Nelson	ISBN: 1-56884-950-8	$9.95 USA/$12.95 Canada
GROUPWARE/INTEGRATED			
Microsoft® Office 4 For Windows®			
For Dummies® Quick Reference	by Doug Lowe	ISBN: 1-56884-958-3	$9.99 USA/$12.99 Canada
Microsoft® Works 3 For Windows®			
For Dummies® Quick Reference	by Michael Partington	ISBN: 1-56884-959-1	$9.99 USA/$12.99 Canada
INTERNET/COMMUNICATIONS/NETWORKING			
The Internet For Dummies® Quick Reference	by John R. Levine & Margaret Levine Young	ISBN: 1-56884-168-X	$8.95 USA/$11.95 Canada
MACINTOSH			
Macintosh® System 7.5 For Dummies® Quick Reference	by Stuart J. Stuple	ISBN: 1-56884-956-7	$9.99 USA/$12.99 Canada
OPERATING SYSTEMS:			
DOS			
DOS For Dummies® Quick Reference	by Greg Harvey	ISBN: 1-56884-007-1	$8.95 USA/$11.95 Canada
UNIX			
UNIX® For Dummies® Quick Reference	by John R. Levine & Margaret Levine Young	ISBN: 1-56884-094-2	$8.95 USA/$11.95 Canada
WINDOWS			
Windows 3.1 For Dummies®			
Quick Reference, 2nd Edition	by Greg Harvey	ISBN: 1-56884-951-6	$8.95 USA/$11.95 Canada
PCs/HARDWARE			
Memory Management For Dummies® Quick Reference	by Doug Lowe	ISBN: 1-56884-362-3	$9.99 USA/$12.99 Canada
PRESENTATION/AUTOCAD			
AutoCAD For Dummies® Quick Reference	by Ellen Finkelstein	ISBN: 1-56884-198-1	$9.95 USA/$12.95 Canada
SPREADSHEET			
1-2-3 For Dummies® Quick Reference	by John Walkenbach	ISBN: 1-56884-027-6	$8.95 USA/$11.95 Canada
1-2-3 For Windows® 5 For Dummies® Quick Reference	by John Walkenbach	ISBN: 1-56884-957-5	$9.95 USA/$12.95 Canada
Excel For Windows For Dummies®			
Quick Reference, 2nd Edition	by John Walkenbach	ISBN: 1-56884-096-9	$8.95 USA/$11.95 Canada
Quattro Pro 6 For Windows®			
For Dummies® Quick Reference	by Stuart J. Stuple	ISBN: 1-56884-172-8	$9.95 USA/$12.95 Canada
WORD PROCESSING			
Word For Windows® 6 For Dummies® Quick Reference	by George Lynch	ISBN: 1-56884-095-0	$8.95 USA/$11.95 Canada
Word For Windows® For Dummies® Quick Reference	by George Lynch	ISBN: 1-56884-029-2	$8.95 USA/$11.95 Canada
WordPerfect 6.1 For Windows® For Dummies®			
Quick Reference, 2nd Edition	by Greg Harvey	ISBN: 1-56884-966-4	$9.99 USA/$12.99/Canada

For scholastic requests & educational orders please
Educational Sales at 1. 800. 434. 2086

FOR MORE INFO OR TO ORDER, PLEASE CALL ▶ 800 762 2974

For volume discounts & special orders please
call Tony Real, Special Sales, at 415. 655. 3048

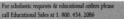

Windows® 3.1 SECRETS™
by Brian Livingston

ISBN: 1-878058-43-6
$39.95 USA/$52.95 Canada

Includes software.

MORE Windows® 3.1 SECRETS™
by Brian Livingston

ISBN: 1-56884-019-5
$39.95 USA/$52.95 Canada

Includes software.

Windows® GIZMOS™
by Brian Livingston
& Margie Livingston

ISBN: 1-878058-66-5
$39.95 USA/$52.95 Canada

Includes software.

Windows® 3.1 Connectivity SECRETS™
by Runnoe Connally,
David Rorabaugh, & Sheldon Hall

ISBN: 1-56884-030-6
$49.95 USA/$64.95 Canada

Includes software.

Windows® 3.1 Configuration SECRETS™
by Valda Hilley & James Blakely

ISBN: 1-56884-026-8
$49.95 USA/$64.95 Canada

Includes software.

Internet SECRETS™
by John Levine
& Carol Baroudi

ISBN: 1-56884-452-2
$39.99 USA/$54.99 Canada

Includes software.

Internet GIZMOS™ For Windows®
by Joel Diamond, Howard Sobel,
& Valda Hilley

ISBN: 1-56884-451-4
$39.99 USA/$54.99 Canada

Includes software.

Network Security SECRETS™
by David Stang
& Sylvia Moon

ISBN: 1-56884-021-7
Int'l. ISBN: 1-56884-151-5
$49.95 USA/$64.95 Canada

Includes software.

PC SECRETS™
by Caroline M. Halliday

ISBN: 1-878058-49-5
$39.95 USA/$52.95 Canada

Includes software.

WordPerfect® 6 SECRETS™
by Roger C. Parker
& David A. Holzgang

ISBN: 1-56884-040-3
$39.95 USA/$52.95 Canada

Includes software.

DOS 6 SECRETS™
by Robert D. Ainsbury

ISBN: 1-878058-70-3
$39.95 USA/$52.95 Canada

Includes software.

Paradox 4 Power Programming SECRETS,™ 2nd Edition
by Gregory B. Salcedo
& Martin W. Rudy

ISBN: 1-878058-54-1
$44.95 USA/$59.95 Canada

Includes software.

Paradox 5 For Windows® Power Programming SECRETS™
by Gregory B. Salcedo
& Martin W. Rudy

ISBN: 1-56884-085-3
$44.95 USA/$59.95 Canada

Includes software.

Hard Disk SECRETS™
by John M. Goodman, Ph.D.

ISBN: 1-878058-64-9
$39.95 USA/$52.95 Canada

Includes software.

WordPerfect® 6 For Windows® Tips & Techniques Revealed
by David A. Holzgang
& Roger C. Parker

ISBN: 1-56884-202-3
$39.95 USA/$52.95 Canada

Includes software.

Excel 5 For Windows® Power Programming Techniques
by John Walkenbach

ISBN: 1-56884-303-8
$39.95 USA/$52.95 Canada

Includes software.

...SECRETS

IDG WORLD TECHNICAL BOOKS

For scholastic requests & educational orders please call Educational Sales at 1. 800. 434. 2086

FOR MORE INFO OR TO ORDER, PLEASE CALL ▶ 800. 762. 2974

For volume discounts & special orders please call Tony Real, Special Sales, at 415. 655. 3048

"A lot easier to use than the book Excel gives you!"

Lisa Schmeckpeper, New Berlin, WI, on PC World Excel 5 For Windows Handbook

Official Hayes Modem Communications Companion
by Caroline M. Halliday

ISBN: 1-56884-072-1
$29.95 USA/$39.95 Canada

Includes software.

1,001 Komputer Answers from Kim Komando
by Kim Komando

ISBN: 1-56884-460-3
$29.99 USA/$39.99 Canada

Includes software.

PC World DOS 6 Handbook, 2nd Edition
by John Socha, Clint Hicks, & Devra Hall

ISBN: 1-878058-79-7
$34.95 USA/$44.95 Canada

Includes software.

PC World Word For Windows® 6 Handboo
by Brent Heslop
& David Angell

ISBN: 1-56884-054-3
$34.95 USA/$44.95 Canada

Includes software.

PC World Microsoft® Access 2 Bible, 2nd Edition
by Cary N. Prague
& Michael R. Irwin

ISBN: 1-56884-086-1
$39.95 USA/$52.95 Canada

Includes software.

BESTSELLER!

PC World Excel 5 For Windows® Handbook, 2nd Edition
by John Walkenbach
& Dave Maguiness

ISBN: 1-56884-056-X
$34.95 USA/$44.95 Canada

Includes software.

PC World WordPerfect® 6 Handbook
by Greg Harvey

ISBN: 1-878058-80-0
$34.95 USA/$44.95 Canada

Includes software.

QuarkXPress For Windows® Designer Handbook
by Barbara Assadi
& Galen Gruman

ISBN: 1-878058-45-2
$29.95 USA/$39.95 Canada

Official XTree Companion, 3rd Edition
by Beth Slick

ISBN: 1-878058-57-6
$19.95 USA/$26.95 Canada

NATIONAL BESTSELLER!

PC World DOS 6 Command Reference and Problem Solver
by John Socha
& Devra Hall

ISBN: 1-56884-055-1
$24.95 USA/$32.95 Canada

NATIONAL BESTSELLER!

Client/Server Strategies™: A Survival Guide for Corporate Reengineers
by David Vaskevitch

ISBN: 1-56884-064-0
$29.95 USA/$39.95 Canada

SUPER STAR

"PC World Word For Windows 6 Handbook is very easy to follow with lots of 'hands on' examples. The 'Task at a Glance' is very helpful!"

Jacqueline Martens,
Tacoma, WA

"Thanks for publish this book! It's the best money I've sp this year!"

Robert D. Templeton,
Ft. Worth, TX, on MORE
Windows 3.1 SECRETS

For scholastic requests & educational orders please
call Educational Sales at 1. 800. 434. 2086

FOR MORE INFO OR TO ORDER, PLEASE CALL ▶ 800. 762. 2974

For volume discounts & special orders plea
call Tony Real, Special Sales, at 415. 655. 3

Macworld® Mac® & Power Mac SECRETS, 2nd Edition
by David Pogue & Joseph Schorr

HOT!

This is the definitive Mac reference for those who want to become power users! Includes three disks with 9MB of software!

ISBN: 1-56884-175-2
$39.95 USA/$54.95 Canada
Includes 3 disks chock full of software.

WINNERS 1994–95
TECHNICAL PUBLICATIONS AND ART COMPETITIONS OF THE SOCIETY FOR TECHNICAL COMMUNICATION

NEWBRIDGE BOOK CLUB SELECTION

Macworld® Mac® FAQs™
by David Pogue

HOT!

Written by the hottest Macintosh author around, David Pogue, Macworld Mac FAQs gives users the ultimate Mac reference. Hundreds of Mac questions and answers side-by-side, right at your fingertips, and organized into six easy-to-reference sections with lots of sidebars and diagrams.

ISBN: 1-56884-480-8
$19.99 USA/$26.99 Canada

Macworld® System 7.5 Bible, 3rd Edition
by Lon Poole

ISBN: 1-56884-098-5
$29.95 USA/$39.95 Canada

NATIONAL BESTSELLER!

Macworld® ClarisWorks 3.0 Companion, 3rd Edition
by Steven A. Schwartz

ISBN: 1-56884-481-6
$24.99 USA/$34.99 Canada

NATIONAL BESTSELLER!

Macworld® Complete Mac® Handbook Plus Interactive CD, 3rd Edition
by Jim Heid

BMUG
SPRING 1994 CHOICE PRODUCT

ISBN: 1-56884-192-2
$39.95 USA/$54.95 Canada
Includes an interactive CD-ROM.

NEWBRIDGE BOOK CLUB SELECTION

Macworld® Ultimate Mac® CD-ROM
by Jim Heid

ISBN: 1-56884-477-8
$19.99 USA/$26.99 Canada
CD-ROM includes version 2.0 of QuickTime, and over 65 MB of the best shareware, freeware, fonts, sounds, and more!

Macworld® Networking Bible, 2nd Edition
by Dave Kosiur & Joel M. Snyder

ISBN: 1-56884-194-9
$29.95 USA/$39.95 Canada

Macworld® Photoshop 3 Bible, 2nd Edition
by Deke McClelland

ISBN: 1-56884-158-2
$39.95 USA/$54.95 Canada
Includes stunning CD-ROM with add-ons, digitized photos and more.

NEW!

WINNERS 1994–95
TECHNICAL PUBLICATIONS AND ART COMPETITIONS OF THE SOCIETY FOR TECHNICAL COMMUNICATION

Macworld® Photoshop 2.5 Bible
by Deke McClelland

ISBN: 1-56884-022-5
$29.95 USA/$39.95 Canada

NATIONAL BESTSELLER!

Macworld® FreeHand 4 Bible
by Deke McClelland

ISBN: 1-56884-170-1
$29.95 USA/$39.95 Canada

Macworld® Illustrator 5.0/5.5 Bible
by Ted Alspach

ISBN: 1-56884-097-7
$39.95 USA/$54.95 Canada
Includes CD-ROM with QuickTime tutorials.

M A C W O R L D ® P R E S S

10/09/9

"Macworld Complete Mac Handbook Plus CD covered everything I could think of and more!"

Peter Tsakiris, New York, NY

"Very useful for PageMaker beginners and veterans alike—contains a wealth of tips and tricks to make you a faster, more powerful PageMaker user."

Paul Brainerd, President and founder, Aldus Corporation

"Thanks for the best computer book I've ever read— *Photoshop 2.5 Bible.* **Best $30 I ever spent. I** *love* **the detailed index....Yours blows them all out of the water. This is a great book. We must enlighten the masses!"**

Kevin Lisankie, Chicago, Illinois

"Macworld Guide to ClarisWorks 2 **is the easiest com- puter book to read that I have ever found!"**

Steven Hanson, Lutz, FL

"...thanks to the *Macworld Excel 5 Companion,* **2nd Edition occupying a permanent position next to my com- puter, I'll be able to tap more of Excel's power."**

Lauren Black, Lab Director, Macworld Magazine

**Macworld®
QuarkXPress
3.2/3.3 Bible**
*by Barbara Assadi
& Galen Gruman*

ISBN: 1-878058-85-1
$39.95 USA/$52.95
Canada
Includes disk with
QuarkXPress XTensions
and scripts.

**Macworld®
PageMaker 5 Bible**
by Craig Danuloff

ISBN: 1-878058-84-3
$39.95 USA/$52.95 Canada
Includes 2 disks with
PageMaker utilities, clip art,
and more.

**Macworld®
FileMaker Pro
2.0/2.1 Bible**
by Steven A. Schwartz

ISBN: 1-56884-201-5
$34.95 USA/$46.95
Canada
Includes disk with ready-t
run data bases.

**Macworld®
Word 6 Companion,
2nd Edition**
by Jim Heid

ISBN: 1-56884-082-9
$24.95 USA/$34.95 Canada

NEWBRIDGE
BOOK CLUB
SELECTION

**Macworld®
Guide To Microsoft®
Word 5/5.1**
by Jim Heid

ISBN: 1-878058-39-8
$22.95 USA/$29.95 Canada

**Macworld®
ClarisWorks 2.0/2.
Companion,
2nd Edition**
by Steven A. Schwartz

ISBN: 1-56884-180-9
$24.95 USA/$34.95 Can

**Macworld® Guide To
Microsoft® Works 3**
by Barrie Sosinsky

ISBN: 1-878058-42-8
$22.95 USA/$29.95 Canada

**Macworld®
Excel 5 Companion,
2nd Edition**
*by Chris Van Buren
& David Maguiness*

ISBN: 1-56884-081-0
$24.95 USA/$34.95 Canada

NEWBRIDGE
BOOK CLUB
SELECTION

**Macworld® Guide T
Microsoft® Excel 4**
by David Maguiness

ISBN: 1-878058-40-1
$22.95 USA/$29.95 Can

Microsoft is a registered trademark of Microsoft Corporation. Macworld is a registered trademark of International Data Group, Inc.

For scholastic requests & educational orders please
call Educational Sales at 1. 800. 434. 2086

FOR MORE INFO OR TO ORDER, PLEASE CALL ▶ 800 . 762 . 2974

For volume discounts & special orders plea
call Tony Real, Special Sales, at 415. 655. 3

10/09/95

**naughorized Windows®
5: A Developer's
uide to Exploring
he Foundations of
/indows "Chicago"**
Andrew Schulman

BN: 1-56884-169-8
9.99 USA/$39.99 Canada

**Unauthorized Windows®
95 Developer's
Resource Kit**
by Andrew Schulman

ISBN: 1-56884-305-4
$39.99 USA/$54.99 Canada

Best of the Net
by Seth Godin

ISBN: 1-56884-313-5
$22.99 USA/$32.99 Canada

**Detour: The Truth About
the Information
Superhighway**
by Michael Sullivan-Trainor

ISBN: 1-56884-307-0
$22.99 USA/$32.99 Canada

**PowerPC Programming
For Intel Programmers**
by Kip McClanahan

ISBN: 1-56884-306-2
$49.99 USA/$64.99 Canada

**Foundations™ of Visual
C++ Programming For
Windows® 95**
by Paul Yao & Joseph Yao

ISBN: 1-56884-321-6
$39.99 USA/$54.99 Canada

**Heavy Metal™ Visual
C++ Programming**
by Steve Holzner

ISBN: 1-56884-196-5
$39.95 USA/$54.95 Canada

**Heavy Metal™ OLE
2.0 Programming**
by Steve Holzner

ISBN: 1-56884-301-1
$39.95 USA/$54.95
Canada

**tus Notes Application
evelopment Handbook**
Erica Kerwien

N: 1-56884-308-9
.99 USA/$54.99 Canada

**The Internet Direct
Connect Kit**
by Peter John Harrison

ISBN: 1-56884-135-3
$29.95 USA/$39.95 Canada

**Macworld® Ultimate
Mac® Programming**
by Dave Mark

ISBN: 1-56884-195-7
$39.95 USA/$54.95 Canada

**The UNIX®-Haters
Handbook**
*by Simson Garfinkel, Daniel
Weise, & Steven Strassmann*

ISBN: 1-56884-203-1
$16.95 USA/$22.95 Canada

Learn C++ Today!
by Martin Rinehart

ISBN: 1-56884-310-0
34.99 USA/$44.99 Canada

Type & Learn™ C
by Tom Swan

ISBN: 1-56884-073-X
34.95 USA/$44.95 Canada

**Type & Learn™
Windows® Programming**
by Tom Swan

ISBN: 1-56884-071-3
34.95 USA/$44.95 Canada

ORDER FORM

Order Center: **(800) 762-2974** *(8 a.m.–6 p.m., EST, weekdays)*

10/09/9

Quantity	ISBN	Title	Price	Total

Shipping & Handling Charges

	Description	First book	Each additional book	Total
Domestic	Normal	$4.50	$1.50	$
	Two Day Air	$8.50	$2.50	$
	Overnight	$18.00	$3.00	$
International	Surface	$8.00	$8.00	$
	Airmail	$16.00	$16.00	$
	DHL Air	$17.00	$17.00	$

*For large quantities call for shipping & handling charges.
**Prices are subject to change without notice.

Ship to:

Name _____

Company _____

Address _____

City/State/Zip _____

Daytime Phone _____

Payment: ☐ Check to IDG Books Worldwide (US Funds Only)

☐ VISA ☐ MasterCard ☐ American Express

Card # _____ Expires _____

Signature _____

Subtotal _____

CA residents add
applicable sales tax _____

IN, MA, and MD
residents add
5% sales tax _____

IL residents add
6.25% sales tax _____

RI residents add
7% sales tax _____

TX residents add
8.25% sales tax _____

Shipping _____

Total _____

Please send this order form to:
IDG Books Worldwide, Inc.
7260 Shadeland Station, Suite 100
Indianapolis, IN 46256

Allow up to 3 weeks for delivery.
Thank you!